IN DEFENSE OF TEENAGERS

Beata Hittrich

A story book written for educators, parents
and above all for teenagers.

"In education, it is my experience that those
lessons which we learn from teachers who are
not just good, but also show affection for students, go deep into our minds. Lessons from
other sorts of teachers may not. Although you
may be compelled to study and may fear the
teacher, the lessons may not sink in. Much
depends on the affection from the teacher."

His Holiness the 14th Dalai Lama

Note for Librarians: a cataloguing record for this book that includes Dewey Decimal Classification and US Library of Congress numbers is available from the Library and Archives of Canada. The complete cataloguing record can be obtained from their online database at:
www.collectionscanada.ca/amicus/index-e.html
ISBN 1-4120-4910-5
Printed in Victoria, BC, Canada

TRAFFORD

Offices in Canada, USA, Ireland, UK and Spain
This book was published *on-demand* in cooperation with Trafford Publishing. On-demand publishing is a unique process and service of making a book available for retail sale to the public taking advantage of on-demand manufacturing and Internet marketing. On-demand publishing includes promotions, retail sales, manufacturing, order fulfilment, accounting and collecting royalties on behalf of the author.
Book sales for North America and international:
Trafford Publishing, 6E–2333 Government St.,
Victoria, BC v8t 4p4 CANADA
phone 250 383 6864 (toll-free 1 888 232 4444)
fax 250 383 6804; email to orders@trafford.com
Book sales in Europe:
Trafford Publishing (uk) Ltd., Enterprise House, Wistaston Road Business Centre,
Wistaston Road, Crewe, Cheshire cw2 7rp UNITED KINGDOM
phone 01270 251 396 (local rate 0845 230 9601)
facsimile 01270 254 983; orders.uk@trafford.com
Order online at:
www.trafford.com/robots/04-2718.html

10 9 8 7 6 5 4 3 2

CONTENTS

I would like to thank my friend Sue Hellman for her generosity in editing my book and to thank my daughter-in-law, Elizabeth who put long hours of work into reading my messy writing and typing the whole manuscript over and over. Also special thanks to my friend Samaya Ryane for polishing it off. Last, but not least, my daughter Anna, without her support, encouragement and loving help this book would never have been finished.

Note: All the stories are true, all persons are real, only a few names have been changed, mainly those whom I could not contact to ask their permission.

I have no intention to add to the volume of books already written about education. This is rather a storybook - true tales about my childhood, my teenage years, and why and how I became a teacher. It tells the story of my children and, above all, the stories of my students.

I have written this book for teenagers and their parents in hopes that by reading it they will gain more understanding and tolerance towards each other. I do not claim to know it all - to have all the answers for the problems of growing up or for the difficulties of raising another human being. I do hope only that reading about my experiences and my views will help reduce the generation gap.

I ask all of you who work in the education system to please excuse me if I do not use the common educational jargon. I have written in the language I speak - keeping it simple as it flows from my heart. Those of you who are looking for a highly sophisticated academic structure within my suggestions about improving education should put the book down and quit reading.

If I can lessen the discomfort and confusion that resides in the teenage soul and open the minds of those who deal with young people, I will have fulfilled my aim in the defense of my beloved teenagers.

Very few of us grow up as obedient, dutiful children who respect our parents and teachers and follow the well-meant advice of those authorities unquestioningly. Most of us want to form our own opinions on everything. Instead of obeying, we explore, earning the labels 'rowdy', 'rebellious', and 'problem child'. To a teenager, the more dangerous the exploration is, the more interesting it seems.

The hardest job of parent-hood begins when your beloved, sweet, little baby becomes thirteen, fourteen, or fifteen. Suddenly you lose your influence. How do you maintain contact and continue to communicate? How will you guide that young person through all the dangers of alcohol, drugs, and early sex? How can you fight the influence of your children's peers and the gangs they associate with?

If you take a hard-handed approach, you risk losing right from the start. "As long as you are eating my bread and living under my roof, you must obey the rules of this house . . . or else!". Very few young people can be kept on the right track by their parents' threats. They are more likely to rebel. "Everyone else is out having a good time, why can't I? The gang is doing all those great things, and I can't be part of it, because of my parent's stupid rules!"

So this young person concludes: "My parents do not understand me. They're old-fashioned. They do not love me, so why should I love them?" The next step is: "I hate my Mom; I hate my Dad."

Students in my art classes talk freely while working on their art projects. Far too often I hear the frightening remark: "I hate my Mom." I stop and ask, "Why do you say that?" The answer is always the same. "She does not understand me. She does not let me do what I want to do."

Young people at this early age do not comprehend the intentions of their parents or the anguish and fear their parents feel for their safety. The only way teenagers know how to respond to the hard-handed approach is with stubborn, equally hard rejection.

What is the answer? When everything else seems to have failed, there is only one: the love approach. "No matter what you do, my son or daughter, I love you." Make your children feel that love. It is not enough just to say it. You must demonstrate it in every way.

First, show interest in everything they do. When they 'party' or play loud music, show interest in their friends. Ask about the boyfriends or girlfriends they choose and the problems that come with these relationships. Even take an interest in their smoking and drinking.

Try to show some tolerance towards their interests, regardless of how far your life and interests lie from theirs. Let your child know you have weaknesses too: you may be a smoker; you may drink, gamble or overeat yourself; or you may watch movies with violence and sex in them.

No matter how conservative a person you are - how strong your moral base is; at some time in your life you must have had to fight certain weaknesses. Do not hide this from your teenager! Do not try to present yourself as perfect, or worse yet, do not cover up your problems with lies. Speak about your own struggle with life and moral values so your child can see you share this experience. If you have ever done something that was not in your best interest, discuss it with your teen-age son or daughter. Looking perfect and making him feel inferior just increases the gap between you. Try to present yourself as a friend instead of the authority figure that you actually are.

You are not going to lose your child's respect in the light of the truth. Quite the contrary. Talk about your worries honestly. Tell your children you are concerned because you love them so much. Say that you are not going to stop loving them whatever they decide to do. Ask them just to think their actions through first. Point out the dangers of their choices, but make them understand you are there with love and support whatever the outcome.

My Grandmother told me a fairy-tale when I was a child. It is a crude, horrible story, as most of the old children's tales are. (Remember the Wolf who ate Grandma and Little Red Riding Hood and the witch who wanted to cook Hansel and Gretel?) Still this story has a lesson to teach, so please listen to it.

A young man who hated his Mother killed her and cut her heart out. (Don't faint. The wicked stepmother in Snow White had the same intention!) He headed into the depth of a dark forest to bury the heart, but as he was walking and holding his Mother's heart in his hand, he tripped over an old root and fell. Stumbling and trying to regain his balance, he heard a voice - the voice of his Mother's heart saying to him: "Oh, my son, I hope you did not hurt yourself."

My Grandmother's message to me was this is how a Mother's heart should be. It should give love and more love despite the actions of the son or daughter. This absolute, unconditional love should be shown every day and in every way possible.

Sooner or later, the young person will end his quest to conquer life and realize: "I am hurting the person who loves me so much!" Parental love may just stop him from doing outrageous things and hurting himself in the process.

Young people do not understand that behind the parent's hard hand is love. They only see the fist, so try showing your love first. When your child falls, pick him up and ask, "Did you hurt yourself?" If your love does not stop the child, keep on with it even if she or he commits a crime. Who is going to care if not you? Who is going to help, if not you?

It is only too late to show your love when your son or daughter commits suicide. More young people contemplate ending their lives than parents can imagine. Such children have lost self-respect. They feel so rejected that they can't bear it any longer. They think they are worthless. They can't face themselves and can't face their parents' disapproval. When everything fails, this is the only way they can show how 'love sick' they feel.

Give your love *now*, not when it is too late.

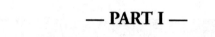

— PART I —

•••

CHAPTER I

•••

"I am not a loser, but you are a f-----n' bitch". With a loud cry, Tom slammed the art room door and disappeared down the hallway.

Thirty Grade 10 students froze in surprise and looked at me with questioning eyes. "What are you going to do, Ms. H?"

Well, I was stunned for a minute, since that kind of outburst only happened once before during my three decades of teaching in high school.

"I feel sorry for Tom," I said, finally. "He must be very frustrated and certainly has chosen a drastic way to express his feelings."

"Will you suspend him?" somebody asked. "I do not think so. Suspension will only give him a reason to feel that way."

The class worked on their painting assignment in deep silence until the bell. At break the vice principal called me to her office. There was Tom sitting like a skinny ruffled bird, looking angry and defensive.

My friend, Mrs. W, the best vice principal I ever had, looked at me and Tom with a very serious expression. "Tom said you called him a loser!" she said. "Is it true?"

I turned toward my student. "I apologize if you understood it that way. What I really said was that you are a capable young man, able to do very good work, but didn't hand in several assignments and sat there socializing instead of painting. I pointed out that as a result I must fail you and asked, why do you set yourself up to be a loser? I may have chosen a very wrong word, but you swore at me and that was a very strong reaction also. I meant to shake you up, because I care!"

"Will I get a suspension?" Tom asked. Mrs. W. looked at me questioningly.

"No, Tom. You stay and think about what I said".

"Sorry," he murmured under his breath.

"That's O.K. son," I answered. "You can't hurt me, I already made it in life, but your whole life is ahead and it's what you make of it now that counts. Failing a fun subject like art is not a good start."

Tom came to class the next day and started to work on a minimal level to pass. We never spoke about this incident again.

This was my last year of teaching before I retired. The following year, I visited my old school to give workshops as part of the annual Global Issues week. As I parked down behind the school, a group of students were gathered around the smoke pit. Our young man Tom was among them. His face lit up as he saw me walk toward the school. He ran to meet me and embraced in an awkward hug. "Ms. H, I miss you!" he said. "I am missing you too Tom and I miss all the others."

I had to swallow my tears, not to show how true my statement was. Retirement is a big change after a lifetime of teaching. I have walked a long and rocky road to get here, where I can see, that the road must end. I am grateful that I had the inner wisdom to cherish every step I took and now have time to share my story with those, who are just starting the journey!

•••

CHAPTER II

•••

At the age of thirteen, I was skinny, undernourished and consequently hungry all the time. It was 1948, a few years after the Second World War had ended. I lived in Budapest, Hungary, where Stalin's Communism had just started to blossom into the horror and injustice of the years to come.

I had big dreams; that gave me energy. I would change the world into a better one, where no terror, no fear, and no hunger would exist - all by myself, of course. Nothing to it! I believed in myself.

I thought all I needed to do was find a way to communicate with people and tell them what happiness is all about. My list of happiness went like this: the love of nature, plants, animals, and people; the freedom to be alive and live according to one's own rules, not under the dictates of the Fascists or the Communists. I thought this formula simple enough for anyone to understand. I assumed that after hearing my views, people would shake off all the binding rules that society and foolish beliefs imposed on them.

Find a way to reach them, that's all I had to do. Then, they could see the world with my eyes. The crystal clear stars above the dirty over-polluted city which was still lying in ruins from the destruction of the war would be revealed. People would learn the wisdom of life from the growing flowers and trees, instead of believing in the fanatical ideas of Stalin's Communism that made those people who followed it narrow-minded and cruel and imposed fear and terror on anyone who opposed.

Children have a lot of magic and inner wisdom. God looks through their eyes and is dismayed by the world He/She sees. Only later when society, school, parents, and religions have taught them otherwise, do they lose that pure way of knowing. Once they have learned the values and rules, which bind most adults then, instead of listening to the magical knowledge that they brought from their before-birth existence, they start to repeat conventional slogans like parrots. The adult world makes sure that children do not stay individuals but become part of the mass and adopt its uniform thinking.

At the age thirteen, I still had a lot of that initial God-given wisdom. Caught between the value systems of the crumbling feudalistic society and the new Communist one, I escaped inward. I named my inner world the 'Magic Garden'. When life became too cold and cruel, I would withdraw into this flourishing garden. Millions of flowers grew in its green meadows. All my experiences in the real world and my reactions to these things, became flowers. Light blue ones appeared for my dreams. Pink ones represented my love for my Mom and my friends. Violence and terror grew into dark red, almost black flowers. The desire to change the suffering of the world added bright reds and oranges to the colours in the meadow. These flowers popped up beside me like fire as I walked through my garden - the place I went when I tried to sort out my thoughts and feelings.

It is not my intention to write about politics. The picture I am trying to describe of my early life in Hungary only serves as a background for my reflections upon my feelings as a teenager. Most young people go through a period of alienation. Parents on the North American continent who provide a beautiful home and a relatively safe and easy life for their children cannot understand why their children are discontented. This alienation, however, is quite common to teenagers from many countries and backgrounds. Children living in rural areas wish to live in the city, and the metropolitan life creates a desire to live in the country. The grass always seems greener on the other side of the fence.

When I was thirteen, the city of my birth, Budapest, was still dressed in the wounds of the Second World War. Many houses did not have facades. The pitiful remains of the tenants' belongings including broken tables and pictures hanging askew on the wall were exposed to all who passed by on the street. The burned remains of homes three to four stories high were out of reach. Eventually with heroic efforts, the city was rebuilt. The open walls were closed again hiding the poverty.

The apartments, hundreds of years old, seemed to hold each other up shoulder to shoulder. The factories that were built around and amongst them started up again. Although their chimneys threw dark grey clouds skyward, the dirt soon settled back down on the rows of buildings. The falling soot painted everything a dull and depressing grey. Dirty, beaten garbage cans lined the concrete sidewalks. The large gates of the apartments breathed cold and wet air. An unhealthy air of poverty mixed with the people's sense of fear.

I did not have the few pennies it took to take the street car, so I walked, my heart filled with the desire to see green grass, flowers and trees. Reading books was my only form of entertainment. I daydreamed about North American Indians and the Indian way of life, and I wished to live in the wilderness.

Now, forty years later I know that this is what brought me to British Columbia where I can touch and even hug the tall Douglas Firs and feel at home. So do not be afraid to dream. Do not be afraid to follow your dreams, whatever they are, until you make them real.

•••

CHAPTER III

•••

Some people are born to a profession. They do not have to think about what to do with their lives. They have an inner drive from the beginning, and they follow a path which seems to be written in the stars.

I was born to be a teacher. I never had any doubt about that. I knew I had first to learn the important lessons myself so I would be able to share them later. My life experiences have been the most important source of my education. They taught me efficiently and effectively.

I never imagined teaching meant standing on a platform and lecturing factual material to the ignorant. I have always regarded teaching as a form of communication. To be able to communicate, you must be interested in people. You must understand people, and when they open up to you, you must try to share what you know to help them to know themselves and grow.

Nobody can teach a person who does not want to learn. One must offer something that the learner does not yet have but wishes to possess. You only can give when the other reaches out to receive.

A teacher can be a storehouse of knowledge, a walking encyclopedia, but if she cannot find a way to share this with others then she isn't worth much as a teacher. A good teacher first guides her pupils to find their fields of interest. Then she can offer the knowledge that is required for them to pursue this interest.

Especially in elementary and junior high school, a good teacher must be a friend, a helper, somebody who cares and is interested in the child personally. Those students who become motivated to learn will find the material they need from books, from research, and by really listening to what the teacher has to say.

According to the latest psychological research, all basic learning occurs between birth and the age of five. What were the lessons that I myself learned during these early years?

When I try to recall my infancy, I remember the vivid dreams of my sleeping hours. The waking hours were dream-like as well. My earliest recollections must be from when I was only a few months old because my Mom was holding me with one arm and splashing water with her other arm, as she gave me a bath. I grabbed her housecoat collar for safety with both hands and stared at the dark blue and white pattern of the material of her dress. She had almost-white, blonde hair and looked like a good fairy - slim and fragile.

I also remember looking through the wooden rails of my little bed into a room full of dark furniture. I loved the pattern of the oriental carpet. Later, when I could walk, I hid under the dining table which became a house of my own. I would pull the table cloth around it while enjoying my dreams.

The chestnut trees along our street had big branches with large green leaves that seemed to float backward while my Mother pushed me in my baby carriage. Lying on my back, I stared up at the patches of blue sky that showed between with the leaves. My favourite memories are of walks in the park. White daisies would brush against my face.

Everybody loved me. I was the centre of attention, but something was seriously wrong. Although I stood just three feet high in a group of adults, I felt absolutely equal to everybody else, still they had serious talks only with each other. They spoke to me in baby talk. This hurt my pride. Even their voices would change when they turned the conversation toward me. If I tried to express my opinion, they would laugh and reply with something like: "Oh you sweet little silly-billy." I often asked questions about things they considered 'for adults only'. They would answer with a saying, that I learned to hate (common in Hungary,): "Just because . . . so the trees won't grow as tall as the sky." That was their signal to me that I had touched upon one of the secrets of the adult world.

In Hungary during the 1930's, the outdated feudalistic system still existed. Class distinction and discrimination against all sorts of people including kids were an everyday reality.

I was born into an upper middle class family, where the ladies learned how to play the piano, dance, do embroidery, and play tennis instead of being taught academic subjects. Higher education was reserved for men. They became the heads of their families. My Grandparents believed that the more education a girl received, the greater the danger there would be of her questioning the accepted moral codes. A lady's place was in the home. Her role was to increase her husband's status by being a well-mannered and polite decoration. Upper middle class ladies paid nannies to look after their children. Their nannies were poor village girls, who had to sell their labour to the rich. Nobody expected my Mother to change my diapers or put up with any other inconveniences. My nanny did all the work of child rearing. She was a sweet girl, very good hearted and hard working, but she knew nothing about the psychology of a child. Neither did my Mother.

If I ran into the living room when my Mom had company and she happened to be talking about those "not in front of a child" things, she would immediately switch the conversation into German. I learned to hate the expression "Nicht for dem Kind."

Discipline was another area that caused my pride to suffer. Spanking a child was common. Nobody seemed to think of trying to talk sense to a little person. Childhood mischiefs resulted in punishments that ranged from a slap to forcing me to kneel in the corner with my hands folded behind my back.

One of the most memorable punishments happened because I didn't want to miss the excitement that the early afternoon offered and I resisted taking a nap. My Mother said the big bad wolf was going to come beside my bed and watch me. I closed my eyes, thinking about playing with my ball and swinging in the garden, but it was impossible to sleep, so I peeked to see if my Mom had been telling the truth. Sure enough, I saw a big furry tail hanging from the polished wooden bed rail. Frightened out of my wits, I lay still for an hour, afraid even to breathe. Later I learned that my nanny had dangled my Mother's silver fox stole, the one she wore around her neck when she took a walk in the winter, there.

The psychologists must be right. Most of my basic learning occurred before I went to school. I decided very early I was going to be different when I grew up. I would treat my children as equals; I would talk to them the same way I spoke to everyone else. No 'googoo gaga's'. I would never spank them, but would explain why I wanted them to do what I asked. I would never teach them with fear. Most of all, if they asked a question, I would explain by telling them the true answers - whatever the subject. I would never ever answer: "Just so the trees won't grow as tall as the sky."

Always remembering my humiliating childhood, both as a Mother and as a teacher, I have kept my promises and treated all my children with dignity.

•••

CHAPTER IV

•••

Not everybody is aware of the fact that history is alive and happening around us all the time. Students in Social Studies classes do not see the connection between the present and the events of the past which affect the circumstances in which they live. Good teachers encourage their pupils to explore the present - the everyday lives of people around them - before they study the past.

For example, the contemporary environmental crisis, with the pollution problem and the disappearing ozone layer, seriously affects young people's lives and their future. Using this concern as a starting point would make it much easier to understand the Industrial Revolution and the impact that the technical achievements of the twentieth century will have on the future.

My 'history lessons' started with the real life experience of World War II bombing raids. In 1945 when I was ten, the Russians had surrounded Budapest entrapping both the occupying Germans and the Hungarian civilians. The tenants of the apartment house my family lived in hid in the basement without electricity, water, or food for eight long weeks. About thirty people gathered together on makeshift beds in the wood cellar that was the size of a living room. The only window, just above the street level, was blocked off with sand bags so we had little fresh air or light.

All my family's worldly belongings were left upstairs in our apartment, ready to be lost to the bombs or bullets of low flying fighter planes' rattling machine guns. We spent those weeks in fear, first from the falling bombs, and then from the bands of armed Russians who were hunting and killing the entrapped German soldiers. When the first Russian soldiers searched our building, they took everything which had value to them. My little red leather wrist watch was ripped from my arm. Our radio was stolen from the table leaving us without news and music. It was ten years before we could afford a new one.

That was just the prelude to the later years of Communist takeover, when all my family's wealth was confiscated. We became as poor as the peasant girls who had previously been our family's servants. As a child, I arrived at the conclusion that material things have no value. They belong to us one day and we can lose them in the next. Only life and its experiences are valuable. The things we carry inside ourselves no one can steal from us.

The restricted life we led then was considerably brightened by books. When I was reading I could travel to faraway places. Books were my entertainment, escape, hope, and fulfilment. Reading helped me through all those years. They are still my best friends today. Books and the dramas of my life have taught me more than I ever learned in a school.

Being undernourished and always hungry, my body developed slowly. My posture was poor. My Mother looked at my hunched shoulders, and one day she signed me up for a creative dance class. The old lady who gave the class had been a famous dancer in her youth. She was now trying to make a living by teaching a few dozen, pale-looking, skinny kids in her home. A wooden bench which lined the exercise room hid her old dance costumes. These helped recreate the atmosphere of another world where glamour, music, light, and laughter had once existed.

Learning to dance opened up a new door out of my limited world. I threw myself into the movement with enthusiasm. I imagined myself as a flower and opened my colourful petals toward the sun. I was the flame that leaped from a burning fire. I was a summer fairy wearing a torn red chiffon costume and bringing fruits to the trees. I let my long braids loose and my body flew while I dreamed my dreams and danced to the music of my teacher's ancient piano.

The teacher praised me and called my progress exceptional. However, after a year my Mother could not afford to pay the few forints for the dance class fee and I had to see my teacher to tell her that I must leave the class. She looked at me with sad eyes. "You are so talented. It is a shame to quit." She reached for my trembling fingers. "I have an idea! Would you like to help me to teach the small children? I have noticed you helping the others in your class. I am old and tired. I can use your help! At the same time you could earn the fee for your own classes."

God bless her! That's how I became a teacher's helper at the age of thirteen. More and more she let me take over, first with the children ages three to six, then with the six to ten year olds. I did my job with enthusiasm. I told the children fairy tales and asked them to act these out with movement. They had to imagine their roles as butterflies, birds, or lady bugs and move accordingly. We invented costumes from old curtains for the year end performance. I danced my favourite role as a summer fairy, and the little ones, dressed like flowers, held up a three year old 'honey bee' who was collecting pollen in a basket that hung on her tiny, fat arm.

The same year I also started high school. The classroom lacked heating and had only a few forty watt light bulbs, leaving us in semi-darkness. We kept our winter coats and gloves on in the classroom, rubbing our frozen fingers together so we could write. My lunch in school was the same every day, as was that of most of the other students; two pieces of bread spread with pork lard. Most of the time I had only a meagre dinner waiting for me at home after school. For six whole years I did not eat butter or meat. Vegetables were scarce and only available in the summer. Cooked beans and potatoes were the regular menu.

Did I find this depressing? Not really. I had my dance classes to look forward to and my marvellous books to read. The magic I experienced through reading and dancing found its way into my other forms of self-expression - drawing and literary composition. My essays made me the pride of the class. My drawings were pinned to the display board, and the skills I learned in creative dance made me the best gymnast in P.E. All this fame turned me into a leader.

The high school I attended was originally run by nuns. It was restricted for girls only. In 1948 the Communist government took the responsibility of education away from the Church and I suspect quickly trained teachers to replace the nuns.

My classmates came from various backgrounds. There was a group of girls from school who were considered my special friends. They followed me around, visited my home, and asked my advice about their problems. I wrote their homework. I loved them, and the more help a friend needed the more attention she got from me.

Of those girls, whose parents were professional people who dressed better and ate relatively good lunches, only a few belonged to my gang. You might say I collected all the losers into my group of friends. Girls from single families whose fathers had died or disappeared during the War and girls from low income or no income homes. My friends were a skinny, poorly dressed bunch, all of whom were hungry for attention and love. Being part of my group gave them the feeling that they 'belonged'. We would meet after school, frequently in my home, and organize hikes in the nearby forest. Hiking did not cost a penny but did us all a lot of good by getting us out of the overcrowded, polluted city.

Sitting on the grass in a forest clearing or gathering around a small fire we had built from tree branches, I would let my imagination go wild. I talked about life and death, individual hopes and dreams, the concept of God and the atheistic ideas of the Communist government. We felt we were being ground up between two worlds. Our parents taught us to fear God, the school taught us that the belief in God was only a superstition. We spent long hours talking about all the controversy we had to deal with. I do not know where I got the courage to stand up and talk about the beauty of nature, the value of life, the power of the human will, and the loving help of the Creator. I did it because of the others, because of their need for guidance and direction. It came from my inborn teacher's instinct to help.

My own thirteen-fourteen-fifteen year old self needed help and guidance, too. I desperately wanted somebody who I could turn to for advice. There was nobody around me. My Father had died when I was six. My Mother was left like a lost child after the storm of World War II. She was completely unprepared to work and to look after me and my needs. She did not even know how to cook. Her meals had been prepared for her during the first forty years of her life. Fortunately, I was an only child and born to survive all the hardships. I took over my Mother's role and tried to give her support and encouragement. I asked a neighbour for simple recipes and started to cook plain meals from our minimal food supply.

It was clear to me that, once my Mother had sold the last pieces of her jewelry along with anything else we owned, I would have to earn money. So I presented my problem to my old friend - the creative dance teacher. Her advice to me was to become a folk dance teacher. God bless her and her excellent idea!

The Communist government was trying to establish a new culture along with the new ideology. Folk dancing was an important part of Soviet life, and the Hungarian government copied the Soviet example in everything. Folk culture became the ideal. The Ballet Institute of the Hungarian Opera was sponsoring a new night school where the most skilful applicants quickly learned songs and dances collected from peasants in our villages and in neighbouring countries. This gave me a golden opportunity to earn money, to teach, and to start my life - MY REAL LIFE.

After a movement skill test, I was accepted into the first group of folk dance teachers to be trained! Every evening I went to classes. After the first month, all new teachers were assigned two or three factories on the outskirts of Budapest. There we taught the assembly line workers how to beat their heals together and sing songs of satisfaction with their new Soviet way of life.

What we learned one day, we taught the next, but we were paid for it. I was fifteen and able to support myself and my Mom and Grandma as well. Happiness was being able to buy a piece of sausage for the soup I cooked or a pair of shoes with no holes in the soles. My greatest treat was chocolate bars. I had craved these for years.

This was how I started my teaching career.

•••

CHAPTER V

•••

To be a folk dance teacher and an instructor of adults at my age required quite a lot of confidence on my part.

The workers in the factories were expected to take part in the 'New Cultural Life'. The older people sang in the choir or acted in the drama club, while the younger generation joined the dance groups, spending two nights a week after work practising. After spending eight to ten hours on an assembly line, most of the participants wished to go home instead of learning dance steps. Yet they showed enthusiasm despite their true feelings for it was a time of pretence.

Whenever Stalin's name was mentioned at a meeting, and he was a popular subject, the people all jumped to their feet, clapped their hands, and shouted in unison: "Long live Stalin!" They hid their hatred behind smiling masks.

Dancing after working hours turned out not to be such a terrible thing after all. Our practices brought the young workers together and it was good exercise. Also, the Hungarian folk songs and folk music are truly beautiful, and the whole nation learned to appreciate their heritage.

The ages of my students ranged from sixteen to thirty years, quite a change after the sweet three to ten year olds in my creative dancing classes. I braided my long hair and pinned it up in a bun to look older. Until I learned their names, I addressed my pupils as ladies or gentlemen, or sometimes even as my sons and daughters. I got away with it. Most of them never guessed their teacher was much younger than the youngest student.

At the institute I myself learned the choreography just one step ahead of what I was teaching. This served as an excellent teacher training program for me. I found out more about communication, motivation, and the general interaction among people this way than I ever did many years later at university. I am grateful to those people in the factories. They taught me how to be a teacher. I still have not stopped learning from my students. There is always something new to learn when working with people, and I hope to keep learning right up until my death.

Along with going to night school and teaching dance, I still attended high school during the days. The work load became increasingly difficult to handle. My days were entirely filled. I would get up at seven A.M., and walk to school where I spent the breaks between my classes doing homework from the previous day. I finished at two P.M. and then went to the market. At home, I would quickly cook a simple meal. Afterward I'd hop on the street car to go to my night school dance class. I would finally end the day in the 'cultural room' in one of the factories teaching folk dance. I was lucky to get home by midnight. After a year of shuffling this heavy schedule, I came to the conclusion that it was too much. At the end of grade ten, I quit school and devoted myself to folk dance teaching entirely.

Dropping out of public school did not mean that I gave up my dream to be a classroom teacher. Although my hopes of getting into the university were slim, I signed up to be a correspondence student. This meant I could study on my own and only had to go to the school to write my exams.

The policies of the Communist government were designed to create a group of Communist leaders who came from the working class. Only those who were born into a peasant or proletariat family were allowed the chance to compete for the limited number of spaces that the university offered in each faculty. Being an optimist, I was ready to fight for my right to learn and become a 'real' teacher. 'Real' meant to me a person who was responsible for a few hundred teenagers. To have a job where I could understand, help, motivate, and guide was my dream.

Keeping my dream in mind, I took my textbooks to work with me on the train and studied day and night while waiting in the stations or in the halls of the culture rooms. It took me four years to complete grades eleven and twelve, and by that time I was twenty.

I have already described the general background of the stage that my life's drama was set on. The post-war poverty followed by the terror of Stalin's Communist government ensured that this wasn't the most cheerful setting to grow up in, and my own family life was equally difficult. The problems I experienced at home motivated me more than anything else to enter the teaching profession.

I lived in a two-bedroom apartment with my Grandmother and Mother, both of them widowed. There were no men in the home and no brothers or sisters. My Grandma was a real lady. She never 'preached water and drank wine'. She lived by her high moral standards and expected everyone else to do the same. Her views had their limitations, but her strong will and character did not.

She lived most of her life as the lady of a huge country estate surrounded by servants. She kept her head high even when she was forced to walk out of her home of over thirty years with nothing but a change of clothes. She had nothing in common with the drastically changed Communist world around her and nothing in common with me, for I despised the rules of the old feudalistic system as much as those of the new Communist system. She loved me, but in a distant way. Talking about anything that was personal was considered by her to be in bad taste. There were many unmentionable topics in our home. For example, I didn't dare speak of or ask questions about my developing and changing physical body.

Grandmother often instructed me in an authoritarian voice: "Beata, a real lady keeps her knees closed when sitting. A real lady holds her body straight and her head high. A real lady does not use improper words." There was a long list of no-no's. I was taught the special ways to greet people. This is a delicate and very difficult art in Hungarian because the language distinguishes between classes by using separate forms of the pronoun 'you'. Speech leaves a lot of room to discriminate and hurt.

I was taught to sit, to walk, and to yield to older people. Table manners were a complicated art as well. We ate our simple meals with manners befitting guests of the queen around the royal table. Grandma put two heavy volumes of an encyclopedia under my arm pits to teach me to sit straight and keep my elbows close to my body while eating.

She taught me all the etiquette of the world she was born into. It was quite contradictory to the life I was submerged in on a daily basis. I worked with worthy uneducated people in the factories - unskilled workers who did not know how to hold a knife and fork properly. Yet, it never occurred to me to feel superior to them. In fact, when Grandma delivered one of her lectures I felt like screaming: "I do not want to be a lady. I want to be just another human being!" Fortunately, I never did become a lady according to her definition, but she meant well and I respected her and have treasured the memory of her for a life time.

My Mother was very different from Grandma. Spoiled by her easy life as a child and later as the wife of a well-to-do husband, she could not stand up in the changed world.

I admired Grandma's strength as she bore her fate with dignity and held her head high despite her changed status in life. She had to share the apartment with her daughter and face old age without any financial support. She never complained - never bored anybody with her aches and pains. She would just close her door and say: "Please respect my solitude. I feel slightly ill."

Later during the Hungarian Revolution when everybody tried to hide behind some cover to escape the bullets that were hitting the walls, she calmly sat in her armchair beside the window sewing as she always did. When the Soviet tanks were rolling through the streets below, shaking the apartment buildings right to their foundations, Grandma brushed aside my plea to hide. "Whatever is God's will is what will happen. I am ready," she told me and she did not move.

As much as I looked up to Grandma for her strength. I detested my Mother's weakness. She was small, fragile and very pretty. My Mother felt she was an innocent victim of the Second World War and all that happened after. She cried often, and when she had a migraine, her screams would fill the apartment. She'd just sit helplessly on her bed while her tears flowed endlessly down on to her chest. She deeply mourned her world which had fallen apart and the loss of the big house, the car, the servants, and her high standing in society.

She wished to die, but she was afraid to take her own life though she often talked about it: "This life is not worth living. Let us die together!" It was a horrifying thought to me. I looked forward to every day as a new challenge. I had great expectations, and had decided I was going to be a winner. Every situation offered a new adventure. The last thing I wanted to do was to die. Often after one of my Mother's hysterical scenes, I would wake up in the dead of the night and check the gas stove in the kitchen and the gas heater in the bathroom to see if they were on or off.

In my early teens, I felt the need to share my feelings with my Mom, but she completely rejected my efforts, being constantly preoccupied with her own self pity. I had nobody to turn to, so I read. The books became a substitute for my Mother. They were my advisors, providing me with guidance, and my window on the world outside.

I read the classics of nineteenth century Europe, the Russian classics, and contemporary Hungarian literature. However the book that caught my attention the most was written by a Hungarian man. To me it seemed fictional having little to do with reality, but the story captured my secret dreams. He wrote about nature:

the majestic Rocky Mountains, the beauty of the tall Douglas firs, the music of running rivers, and the thundering waves of the Pacific Ocean. He wrote about the North American Indian Nations that occupied this fantastic world. I was enchanted by every sentence I read.

One day, while visiting a friend, I met the 'writer'. He was thirty-six years of age, with dark eyes, dark skin, and black hair turning white on the temples. In short, he looked like an Indian.

I fell in love instantly, madly, romantically. This first love had nothing to do with physical desire. It was platonic in the purest sense. I knew almost nothing about physical love. No adults considered it important to enlighten our generation with that kind of information. Anyway I was undernourished and skinny like a broomstick. Only my sprit burned with this love which lasted for four years.

This new feeling gave my spirit wings and sweetened my dreams. I felt so overwhelmed, I had to share this with someone, so I told my Mother about my love. She looked at me with surprise and then started to laugh: "How ridiculous it is to talk about love! You are a little girl. What do you know about love at all?"

True enough, my only information regarding the subject had come from the novels I had read. Sex oriented literature was non-existent in Hungary. Books like *Anna Karenina* gave me only a presentiment of what happens between a man and a woman.

I felt deeply hurt by my Mother's laughter. I pulled back into my own world. I promised myself then I would never do that to my children. I would listen and understand.

The ages of thirteen to sixteen are the most difficult years in every child's life. You are not a sweet little girl anymore. Your breasts are developing; you start your period, and with the physical changes, your mental and emotional state change, too.

Lucky are those teenagers who have a mother or a father to talk to. I did not. As lonely as I felt, I discovered that other teenagers around me felt the same way. Most of my classmates and friends felt misunderstood and were without guidance. While I listen to their problems and feelings, my own seemed to fade into the background. While I was helping them and trying to answer their questions, in some mysterious way my problems got solved.

When I felt mixed up and helpless, I would go for long, long walks into the Pilis Mountains. I would talk to the flowers and the trees. I tried to talk to God, but I could not really believe in his existence. I rejected the Communist atheism, but the religious dogmas turned me off too. So I walked, thinking sometimes that I might try living in the forest so I could regain my strength and inner peace. I told myself that there must be an order and a wisdom behind this chaotic life and vowed to find it. I would help myself and others - especially the young ones, to ease their growing pains. One day I would understand the world and everyone in it. I would devote my life to helping people find themselves and their way through the maze.

•••
CHAPTER VI
•••

Through the study of Hungarian folk dances and music I was introduced to the wisdom of the people of the villages. They sing about their lives, their hopes, their loves, and their disappointments. There are many straight forward references to human sexuality. While learning those songs I started to wonder about the physical aspects of love.

My platonic love toward the writer stopped me from looking at the young men around me. I thought that my love for him was eternal. Consequently I wasn't about to fall for anybody else.

Being sixteen and quite pretty, I did receive a lot of attention from the opposite sex. I was asked out on dates more often than any of my friends - not because I was more attractive than other girls, but because my job exposed me to literally hundreds of people. I treated all the boys I knew like friends and nothing more. Those who consistently pursued my company became my closest friends. Two particular boys, a few years senior to me, often came hiking with me. They came with me to the Pilis Mountains for long walks. We slept under the trees or in a cave, rolled up in blankets. (Who had a tent or other such luxuries?) Their cheerful conversations, their jokes, and their loud laughter still echo in my memory to this day. They confessed to me some fifteen years later that they'd wished to court me, but dared not, for my head was stuck high in the clouds.

There was another friend I went to operas and concerts with. He was a music lover. Other young men helped me to cut my firewood in the winter and carried my grocery basket from the market to the third floor of the apartment house I lived in. I was grateful for their attention and friendship, but did not know what to do with their feelings towards me. I found this disturbing and so tried to ignore it.

In night school one of my male classmates, Geza, paid extra attention to me. After classes, he would escort me home through the icy, dirty, dark streets. I was seventeen at the time. Geza's Father had been a high ranking officer in the Hungarian army, during World War II. Now, he was an aging man with a helpless wife, who like my Mother could not adjust to the changed world.

Although Geza came from a family background similar to mine, he supported the Communist ideals enthusiastically. He had read *Das Kapital* and tried to change my opinions by quoting Marx. Consequently we had heated arguments while walking the cold streets. I did not find him attractive at all, but his big blue eyes got to my heart in a strange sentimental way.

In 1952, the government began a tremendous effort to change the old agricultural economy into an industrial one. The poorest people from the countryside found work either right in the capital city or in the many factories that surrounded Budapest. Masses of people moved to the city. However, much of the damage done to the buildings during the war still had not been repaired and there definitely weren't any new housing projects. The shortage of living space grew to frightening proportions.

The Soviet-dictated government tried to solve the problem by forcing undesirable members of society to move out to remote villages and farms. These unwanted people were, of course, the members of the previous ruling society. They had been labelled 'reactionaries'. Most of them had already been imprisoned or were working in labour camps. The A.V.H. (secret police) started to single out the remaining 'enemies' and Gezas' parents were among those unfortunates. My Father had died in 1941, so Mother and myself, unlike my uncles, escaped the forced move. We were permitted to stay in our rented apartment.

The government's move to create housing for the new proletariate created an immense amount of drama in people's lives. The method was always the same. The A.V.H. showed up at the door and presented a written note. The family had a day, or sometimes only a few hours to pack a few clothes and a few personal possessions. The rest of their belongings had to be left behind. Then the army truck took them away. A new family, in good standing with the Communists got their home. There was no one to appeal or protest to. Those who were forcibly moved were still better off than those who disappeared into the A.V.H. prisons forever.

My heart sank when I heard the news from Geza, but he remained positive. He said he understood the intentions of the government, although he wrote a personal letter to the leader of the Communist Party stating that he was a devotee of Communist ideas and asking the officials to please excuse his family and himself from the forced move. Nevertheless, the A.V.H. truck arrived to take the family away. Only Geza was allowed to stay. His family's apartment was to be occupied by a family of five and himself. He could keep one room out of the three and share all the facilities. Because of the housing shortage, the shared rental arrangement was common. A married couple without children was entitled to one room only. This was a necessary, but horrible, solution to the lack of living space.

Geza came to my night class with the good news that he needn't follow his parents and with the bad news that he had been drafted and must leave Budapest to serve for two years in the army. He walked me home as usual. With tears in his eyes he told me how much he loved me and said that all he could take with him was the hope that I might accept his love. I felt sorry for him and gave him a hug. He took it as encouragement and kissed me on the mouth. My first real kiss tasted like salty tears and left my heart heavy with sorrow.

I thought of my ideal love - the 'writer'. He was twenty-two years senior to me, married with a son. I compared his dreams of the virgin forests and the Indian way of life with Geza's dreams of a Communist Hungary where everybody would be 'equal' and the uneducated proletariate would lead the country toward an economic and social miracle that would give everybody enough to eat. In the harsh reality of after war life, both of their dreams seemed unrealistic to me.

Three months later, Geza got his first leave from the army. Instead of visiting his parents on the farm, he showed up at my doorstep. He looked awful. As with all the first year recruits, his curly brown hair had been shaved off leaving a pale scalp that contrasted sharply with his dark, red, frost-bitten ears. His uniform reeked of disinfectant and his boots, weighing several kilograms, rubbed raw blisters on his feet. He looked pitiful, but his big blue eyes burned with the same devotion.

We spent the evening and part of the night together talking about his dreams and hopes. Just before he had to leave, he suddenly said: "You must find me really repulsive. I look terrible, but my heart is aching for you." I wanted to reassure him and show how indifferent I was towards his appearance so I offered him a kiss. One kiss led to another. Suddenly the air got very hot around him and I could not make him stop without hitting him hard or telling him off with harsh words. I was trapped by my own soft-heartedness.

Millions of thoughts ran through my head. What should I do? There seemed no way to get out of this situation. Finally I let it happen. I decided that if I could not be with the man I loved, at least I was with somebody who loved me. Besides, I was curious. I wanted to know what sex really is. So much seemed to pivot around it - novels, songs, poems, jokes.

Geza left happy. He went back to the army and I found myself absolutely stunned: "Is that all? Is that brutal and very physical act the most important part of adult people's lives?" Now I had become an adult myself. I knew the big secret that everybody seemed to hint at, but which nobody talked of in an honest or straightforward way.

I will never forget the next two months. Dark thoughts oppressed me: "What if I am pregnant?" To make the situation worse, my Mother sensed something and asked me if anything had happened between Geza and me. I admitted to the crime. It felt like a crime because my Mother reacted with such horror and disgust. She pulled away from me as if I had leprosy. She avoided even touching me, not to mention hugging or kissing me. She gave me no advice or reassurance of her love and support.

The screaming hysterical scenes between us became an everyday event, especially when the time for my period drew close. The nervous tension must have caused me to skip a cycle. This made us both think I was pregnant. All hell broke loose at home. Still, after almost forty years, if I think about those two months, I feel a cold horror gripping my heart.

It was a hard lesson to learn in life, but I learned it well. I am rather grateful after all. My Mother turned out to be an influential teacher; she modelled for me how not to do things. When my turn came to be a Mother myself, all I had to do in a troubled situation was consider what my Mother would have done, and then act in the opposite manner.

In 1952, abortions were out of the question. What were my alternatives? There was only one. I wrote a letter to Geza, explaining the situation. He asked for a special leave from the army. We went to the registrar's office in a hurry, with only two friends as witnesses, and got married. He returned to the army the same day. I packed up my books, my diary, my stuffed animals, and my few clothes and moved into Geza's shared apartment. Needless to say, a month later my period arrived at the regular time. I was not pregnant, but I was married.

•••

CHAPTER VII

•••

Quitting school had provided me with more free time, and I used this time to take on more dance groups. Real life continued to be my classroom. Through dance teaching I met hundreds of people, young and old, successful ones and failures. I made friends with the assembly line workers and with the presidents of the factories. I got an inside look at the lives of party members, coal miners, and gypsy musicians. I was young, quite pretty and a dance teacher, which was an occupation that was considered quite Bohemian and glamorous. As a result I became a trusted friend to many people.

In 1952-53, the world seemed to be a hopeless and worthless place. Everybody worked for a bare minimum. The Stalin era kept a grip on everything and everybody. Terror, fear, uncertainty, and hunger are the words that best describe those years. The capital was poorly supplied with food. We ate bread and lard most of the time. Everybody dressed poorly. Our wardrobes were composed of old, mended and altered skirts and blouses. Buying a pair of shoes then was more difficult than buying a car is today.

I travelled to every corner of the city as well as to the surrounding mining and industrial settlements. I enjoyed my independence, especially living apart from my Mom, but sharing the same apartment with another family was no fun at all. To tell the truth, it was hellish, not just for me but for all the hundreds of thousands of others who lived in shared rental homes.

Many people rented out one of the two rooms they had to prevent the government from moving unwanted strangers into their homes. This was their only way to choose with whom they would share the kitchen, the bath tub, and the toilet. My Mother rented out my room to a university student.

Those years brought out the best and the worst in everyone. Parents worked ten to twelve hour shifts a day and did not have time or energy for their children. Early morning street cars were filled with tired looking people wearing work clothes and with Mothers who had bundled up babies on their arms. The government had set up kindergartens and daycare centres for young people of all ages from newborns to teenagers. Most of the factories had daycare services, as did all the schools in the city. Children spent long hours in these facilities. In elementary schools, children stayed in the same classroom from seven in the morning till seven at night or until one of their parents picked them up. Those who had a retired grandma who would look after them at home were fortunate.

Schools and homes were poorly heated. The lack of gardens around the apartments and the lack of playing fields around the schools forced young children to stay inside. They were practically locked to their school benches for many years.

Teenagers were luckier. They did not require close supervision anymore, so they could go home on their own to spend the afternoon with homework and housework. The only entertainment they had was to study together. No birthday parties, no television, and no school dances or camping trips brightened their lives. Stereos were unheard of, and the only two stations on the radio beamed out Communist slogans and songs. The movie theatres played poorly made, boring films about the great Soviet way of life.

Sometimes I wonder about those years and whether parents thought about their children's feelings, dreams, and hopes at all. Perhaps putting food on the table and shoes on the little one's feet were the only ways to show they cared.

School was a pretend place where everybody showed enthusiasm towards Communist ideals. Teachers pretended that they believed in the new ideology and the students acted as if they believed what the teacher said.

The government changed all the text books, even the literature had to be selected. Only works which supported the Party were allowed. The rest were labelled worthless, decadent, capitalist, and bourgeois. Overworked, bitter parents talked freely about politics with friends and family members in the security of their homes, while the young ones learned that there are two kinds of worlds that exist: one where you can say the truth about what you think, the other where you lie and pretend in order to for survive. Lying was as necessary to live as eating, and pretence was an art to be mastered. These were not sins, but virtues.

This sad and pitiful new society was maintained by the denial of basic human rights such as individualism and religious freedom. People attended church services in secret or completely stopped going out of fear. Atheism was the basis of the new ideology. Everybody who had religious values was ridiculed. People lost their jobs because of their religious beliefs. One of my classmates was prevented from going to school and deprived of her education because she had committed the crime of giving out pictures of the Virgin Mary to her classmates as a Christmas gift.

Hungarian teenagers of the 50's struggled to build their own set of core beliefs, drawing on whatever their experience proved to be true. Some of my friends secretly prayed the Holy Rosary and sneaked into empty churches for spiritual support. Others like myself read books and thus escaped into the past or into the heroic world of fiction. Geza believed in an idealistic Communist society. He considered all the outrageous actions of the Party as steps necessary to the creation of a rosy idealistic world in which everybody would be equal and would walk hand-in-hand and be selflessly devoted to the well being of the nation.

I found atheism required more unquestioning belief than the dogmas of organized religion. I detested both and turned to books in search of my own truths. I read the Bible twice from the Old Testament to the Gospels. Then I went on to all the available books about other religions of the world. Not finding answers to my questions, I read through heavy volumes by famous philosophers from Imanual Kant to Francis Bacon. I loved the bitter-sharp words of Voltaire and dreamed along with Russeau as he described his vision of a utopian society. Still not satisfied, my inner thirst propelled me to the world of art and classical literature. The masterpieces of the Renaissance enchanted my heart, and Shakespeare's plays opened up new avenues of thought.

I realized that all these philosophers, artists, and writers were pursuing the same road as I was myself. We were searching for truth. We walked a road which seemed to have no end. For a while *Hamlet* was my favourite drama. I compared myself to the troubled Danish Prince.

Despite all the negative aspects of our lives, there was one very positive thing for young people in the 50's: we had meaningful friendships. When we teenagers came together, we rarely spoke about superficial topics. We exchanged ideas and true feelings and tried to help and support each other as we endured the mass confusion of the post-War society.

Sex education was completely lacking in the school curriculum and parents never spoke about the subject at home. This was not such a problem for young people in the villages who had the natural world of animals to teach them what they needed to know about the facts of life. In the capital city, people could not even keep cats in their over-crowded apartments. Parents had grown up in a world where sex was unmentionable and probably did not really know how to enlighten their children. They had enough problems just with everyday survival. As a result, most of them chose not to say anything about sex to their children. The result was a lot of misconception and ignorance.

Those of my friends who had brothers or a Father at home had some ideas. These fortunate youngsters either took notice of their parents sex life because they slept in the same room or pieced together some knowledge from dirty jokes they heard from their brothers. Living with my Mother and Grandmother, I did not have any information and I laughed at my friends' jokes without comprehending them at all. I was always too shy to admit my ignorance.

Seeing my Mother's reaction to anything to do with sex, I formed a false and sad idea. I thought physical love must be shameful and dirty. It took me many years to revise my thinking and to discover beauty and magic in the physical expression of love.

Geza came home for three days on holiday leave. He was happy and full with expectations and plans for our future. The reality of my marriage hit me when I had to share my bed with my 'husband'. I tried to love him back, but the real feelings were missing. Maybe our relationship would have lasted longer if there hadn't been any sex.

Children learning about sex early in their lives have time to get used to the idea because they think about it and fantasize. My dreams about love-making had gotten no further than holding hands with the writer while walking in a moonlit garden.

Geza was blinded with love and left happy after the three days. I had a cold, frightened feeling in my chest. "How am I going to live my life like that? When his two years in the army are over, he is going to be beside me every day. What am I supposed to do?"

Then one day I had a visitor. My heart jumped into my throat when I opened the door. My dream man, the writer, was standing there with flowers in his hands. He explained: "I heard about your marriage and I came to congratulate you personally." "How nice of him," I thought, while I tried to control my shaking hands and offered him a chair and a cup of coffee.

He did not waste much time, but asked immediately about Geza. Satisfied with my answer that my husband was with the army somewhere in the countryside, the writer threw one arm around my waist and grabbed my chin with his other. He kissed my mouth passionately. I was paralysed with surprise when I realized his intentions. He pushed me towards the bed and asked: "What's the matter with you? Haven't you been in love with me for years?"

"Yes," I answered, "I love you, but I am married to Geza now and . . ." "Married," he said, "married, this is good. If anything had happened between us before that it would have been a problem. You were a virgin and I could have gotten you pregnant, but now you are married, so there is nothing to fear. Let's go to bed!"

I felt like somebody had stabbed a knife into my heart. I turned ice cold and pushed him away. I told him to leave at once and forever. When I closed the door behind him, I felt that I had closed the door on my childhood. "Wake up Beata! Wake up from your dream world! He is not the person you imagined. He is just an ordinary man." If I had thrown a ball across the road, I might have hit a better man than this writer about whom I had dreamed for four long years.

I had to sit down and think. I had loved an image which was a creation of my mind. It had nothing to do with reality. What now? My heart was empty. That pure love in me had died, but could I love my husband? For weeks I examined my feelings and arrived at this conclusion: "Geza is a nice young man, but I can only be his friend. Even that is hard considering his beliefs and ideas. Feeling sorry for him is not enough of a foundation for a whole life together."

"When my love for the writer died, my heart became free. I am only seventeen years old. I have my whole life ahead of me. I must get out of this marriage and get a divorce. What about Geza? Talking to him honestly and causing him pain is better for him than pretending to love him when that love doesn't exist.

"I would not have married him if I had not thought I was pregnant or if my Mother had tried to understand and help me instead of pushing me into a desperate solution with her hysterical scenes."

I decided I would teach my own children early about the facts of life. I would try to help them avoid getting married without true feelings of love. To have curiosity or desire when your body has ripened is a natural thing. It is nothing to be ashamed of. I would be sure my children understood their own feelings and that they would never have to hide anything from me. I would not overreact or get hysterical about any revelation that they might make me face.

I gathered up my courage and wrote one letter to Geza and then another to his parents to whom I had regularly been sending money. I explained everything honestly. Geza's reaction was a desperate plea not to leave him. His parents turned against me with anger. I did not blame them for their feelings and continued to send them funds until Geza finished his service. They accepted the money and comforted their hearts with the belief that I had been an 'easy to get' girl. After all I had gone to bed with their son before marriage. I did not deserve their great son. I was probably unable to live without him until the end of his army service because of my hot blooded nature. I became a whore in their eyes. I did not blame them for that. After all, my own Mother did not understand what had happened either.

So I just went ahead with my plans. I hired a lawyer and filed for divorce. Fortunately, getting a divorce then was almost as easy as getting married. Half a year later it was done. The judge had a jovial smile on his face when I stated my reason for ending my marriage: "Your Honour, I was only 17 years old. I was too young to know what I was doing."

In 1953, I moved back to my Mother's apartment. It was completely impossible to get a place of my own. Young couples with children could not get an apartment to live in. In the world of shared rental, there was no choice for a person who wanted to be independent. She had to put up with the inconvenience of either family or strangers, in order to have a roof over her head.

I thought about how much better it would be to be a ground hog. Unlike we humans who inhabit a miserable world of concrete and bricks - an urban hell that we called the capital city - he has his own hole in the ground.

•••

CHAPTER VIII

•••

Being a teenager in the 1950's behind the iron curtain, was not any better or worse than being a teenager in the 80's in America - it was just different. The political pressure, the restrained circumstances, the hunger and lack of comfort in our lives - these helped us learn survival lessons. Living in unheated and over-populated apartments, washing our clothes by hand, wearing shoes with holes in them, and scraping pennies together to buy a cheap candy had a lot to do with shaping our characters.

I remember feeling joy and happiness simply because I was alive, active and challenged. Everybody around me walked more or less in the same boots. Nobody drove a Jaguar or a Porsche or otherwise planted seeds of envy and greed in my heart.

The people of Hungary were united by our poverty, our lack of political free-dom, and our hatred of the Soviet. Talking to other people and having so much in common made us feel better. We agreed on all the basic issues of our lives. While many disappeared into the prisons of the A.V.H., those of us left behind kept on making political jokes. We laughed a lot to escape depression and we called our jokes 'hang-man humour'. We kept our fists clenched tight inside our pockets and were ready to fight for freedom if the opportunity ever arose. This opportunity came a few years later in 1956.

We did not suffer the confusion of today's teenagers who have a million oppor-tunities to choose from. We did not have any opportunities. Private ownership was curtailed by the government. Agriculture, industry, education, and every-thing else was taken over by the state. The Communist slogans stated: "The Proletariate rules! The people own everything. They are working for themselves." In reality everybody became penniless and helplessly surrendered to the Soviet dictatorship.

It may sound controversial, but I think that growing up in that frightening and depressing world was easier than growing up is now. My friends and I felt like comrades in the same battle. Our desperate lives gave us a feeling of heroism.

Travelling on overcrowded street cars and trains, walking in the winter with newspaper stuffed into my shoes to keep my feet warmer and drier, and being hungry most of the time did me a lot of good. It opened my eyes to others' suffering and awoke in me a compassion towards my fellow human beings.

Those circumstances brought out the best and the worst in everybody, and we learned how to tell good people from the bad. Those who helped the Communist government by adding to the oppression of others because they wanted a better position, we did not trust. Those who worked twelve to sixteen hour shifts just to make a few pennies were our friends.

Clearly not everything worked to our advantage, however. The constant need for self-protection in school and in the workplace taught everybody to lie. We had to show enthusiasm for the enforced Communist regime. We used a double standard in everyday conversation, speaking truthfully only to those we trusted. Constant lying does not enhance people's morals. When pretence becomes a necessity and an art, it is hard to teach higher ideals to teenagers. We knew our parents had to fear for their safety and for their lives. Still the images of 'parent' and 'adult' became tarnished.

I remember dreaming of a world where people would be free to speak their minds and debate any opinion. The problem of the 'generation gap' is as old as mankind, but in my youth it was flavoured by the tremendous changes of the society I lived in. The old feudalistic world was based on the moral codes of the Catholic or Protestant churches. The parents and grandparents of my contemporaries could not help but see the world through the feudalistic cultural conditioning of their own youth even though the old society had fallen to pieces under the hammer of the Soviet.

Our parents either clung desperately to the old values or were so shaken by the changes that they fell into despair and disillusionment. Their familiar world and its morals gone, they could not offer guidance to the younger generation. Adults tended to speak in a confusing manner, on one hand praising the old values and expecting their children to follow them while on the other blaming the old values for having failed them. They wondered how God could really exist if he had let all this happen.

My Grandma stood up strongly for religion and the old world morals. My Mother could not believe in anything and gave herself up to despair. She cried and cried, not really knowing what she mourned anymore - the loss of the comfortable life of a lady, her family's lost wealth, or her lost belief in God. Seeing my Mother so weak was the hardest thing I had to bear in my teenage years.

My friends had similar feelings. Most of their fathers had died in the war just like mine or were serving prison terms and had disappeared in Siberia. Those fathers who were still with their families worked day and night and kept their opinions to themselves. The mothers worried more about how to dress and feed their children than about how to feed their hearts and dress their souls.

We young people were growing like weeds in abandoned gardens. Our problems, dreams, hopes, disappointments, and all the big questions about life remained unheard and unanswered. The support that we needed but could not get from parents and teachers, we sought from friendships. I had a few dozen friends, boys and girls, with whom I talked about the questions of life.

I was confident of my own strength and could support myself financially. This made me a leader among my peers. Even if I could not solve their problems, at least I lent a sympathetic ear or a shoulder to cry on.

Slowly I became 'the man' in my family too. I was the one who provided food and clothes and gave advice on every problem. My Mother relied on me in every aspect of our family business from filling out bureaucratic forms to paying the bills.

Crying about the hardships did not help. It was easier just to get through the days with as much optimism and confidence as I could muster. My teen years were a great learning opportunity. They provided me with a solid base for my future teaching career.

My heart fills with gratitude when I recall all those people who shared my life - friends, students, co-workers, and even the people of the streets of the old city. They taught me so much about life and human nature. I would like to embrace all of them - the weak, the desperate, the wise, and the brave. Now, forty years later, I wonder how many of them are alive. Do they have a better life, peace in their hearts, wisdom, happiness?

I would like to write about all of them, but it is impossible. Their stories would fill many books. Through them I learned to love mankind and especially the young people in the troubled stage which we call adolescence.

•••

CHAPTER IX

•••

The poverty of the post-war years did not prevent teenagers from having fun. We did not have sports equipment, stereos, or a place to throw a party, but we had enough imagination to fill the void.

Apartment complexes, with their dark connecting corridors, musty air, and yard gates became childrens' playgrounds. Passersby never knew that a paradise was hidden behind the massive brick walls. A building could become a magical fortress of hallways, staircases and cobblestone courtyards in the minds of the tenants' children. It could turn into an enchanted forest or a pirate ship depending on what game they played. Only the parents saw such places as cold, bare and dark. Having to run to and from work with briefcases and grocery bags under their arms, they had no time to remember their childhood fantasies.

My male hiking companions, Boleny and Sas, lived in the same huge apartment complex. Boleny and Sas both grew to be over six feet tall by the time they reached fifteen. The bread and lard and cooked dry bean diet did not show in the length of their legs, but their frames did not have any fullness. Their skin was stretched thin over their skeletal bones.

Because of their height, they felt out of place among the smaller kids. They did not ask to be included in kid's games of hide and seek or Indian wars, thinking that they had outgrown such pastimes. Boleny and Sas stuck together creating friendship that lasted a lifetime.

The two boys made their own games and mischief. They would laugh for days afterward. For example, one day they tied a long grey string to an empty wallet. They placed the wallet on the sidewalk and ran the string back through the apartment gates. They hid in the yard, lying on their stomachs, and they grinned from ear to ear in expectation.

Three women came around the corner. The wallet caught the eye of the woman in the middle. She pushed the other two aside and pounced with her grabbing hands on the empty sidewalk. Her face reddened with anger and embarrassment while she quickly explained to the others that her intention had been to catch something which seemed to have fallen from the windows above.

Boleny and Sas rolled with laughter for several minutes before they replaced the wallet as bait to catch another innocent passerby. The next victim was an old gentleman who walked with a stick. When he saw the wallet, he stopped. Quickly he glanced left and right, then leaned forward, but the wallet disappeared. He looked again, rubbing his eyes, even putting his glasses on but saw nothing. Disappointed, he walked away, turning to look back several times. The old man touched his head possibly thinking that he must be losing his mind.

After the boys had enjoyed a good laugh, the wallet appeared for a third time to trick the leader of a slightly intoxicated group of factory workers. These men had obviously come from the local pub. The leader marched with his buddies like soldiers, counting every step. When he noticed the wallet, he ordered the happy group to search the sky for clouds. Then he stopped and ordered the others: "All march ahead; I want to see how the last person keeps in line!" The group obeyed. When he quickly turned to pick up his find, the wallet had disappeared. He had no choice then but to run after the others, obviously attributing his vision to the several beers he had consumed.

"Let's go home," said Sas.

"No, wait for one more," asked Boleny, after recovering from his laughing fit.

A little boy was approaching the wallet. He almost tripped over it when he finally noticed the treasure, but it disappeared under the gate. The boy stared at the empty sidewalk and started to cry.

Boleny and Sas stepped out from behind the gate. "Why are you balling your eyes out?" they asked.

"Here, here," sniffed the boy. "I saw a wallet. I swear I did!"

"What did you want to do with it?" they asked.

"Well, if it had a name and address in it, I would have taken it back to the owner who would certainly reward me with some money and I could buy ice cream."

"And what would you do if it did not have an address in it?" asked Sas.

"In that case," said the little boy with glowing eyes, "I would buy ice cream with all the money!" He said that with such enthusiasm it was as if he was already holding the wallet thick with money in his hands.

Boleny reached in his pocket and fished out a two forint coin. "Here, little brother! Go and enjoy an ice cream!" The boy jumped for joy and ran away.

"What an excellent idea!" said Sas. "Let's go and get ourselves ice cream, too."

Boleny slapped his empty pocket with resignation. "Impossible! That two forint was meant to buy an exercise book for school. I don't have a penny more, but I'll have a lot to explain when my mother finds out that I didn't spend the money the way she expected."

Marg and Sue were my classmates from grade seven to grade ten. During those four years, we spent most of our lunch periods together, walking the corridors of the old school building or sitting on the staircase. We always had the same lunches. Marg and Sue brought lard spread between two pieces of bread and I had a dark, thickly cooked, plum jam sandwich. My family had a few large jars left from when we had canned the fruit from Grandma's orchard. The orchard had long since been swallowed up by the state farms.

Everyday Marg, Sue, and I opened our lunches expecting by some miracle to find cheese, sausage, or cold cuts. Of course it never happened, so we shared what we did have, first eating the bread and lard and saving the plum jam sandwich for dessert.

Unlike some of the others in the class of fifty-six students, none of us three girls had a father to bring home an income. Clare, a classmate whose father was a doctor, brought ham sandwiches, apples, and other delicacies we could only dream about in her lunches. I will never forget the scrambled egg sandwiches she ate. I craved them for years. One egg cost 3.50 forint. That was equal to an hour's pay. I couldn't even afford eggs when I started to earn my living.

One day Clare brought an orange to school. The whole class went wild with desire. She generously split the orange into segments, sharing each with a close friend. The rest of us got a little piece from the peel. We accepted it with gratitude. The pleasure I got while I smelled the little orange peel was enormous. I pressed it between my fingers for an hour, enjoying the fragrance of the oil it gave off. Little by little, half millimetre by half millimetre, I ate the exotic delight while imagining the blue Mediterranean sky and a sea shore lined with orange trees.

One day, Marg slammed her lard sandwich to the floor. "I am tired of it! I would like to eat sausage or salami." She almost cried. Sue quietly chewed on her bread. "Does it matter what you eat?" she asked with wise resignation of an old philosopher. "The aim is to fill your stomach, to kill the hunger. After you have finished, you can imagine that you ate fried chicken or anything else you desire!" We laughed a lot over her suggestion.

From that day on we asked each other at every lunch, "What are you eating today?" "Oh, I have roast beef!" "And what do you have?" "I am being thrifty today. I only brought salmon and caviar."

Sue's idea really worked. It brightened up every lunch time. It inspired us to make up wild food fantasies which served two purposes. We forgot our misery and we laughed a lot at each other's hilarious ideas.

The game took new turns every day. We decided to go into business and open up a 'restaurant' where we could display paper mach'e imitations for all the menu items. The name of the place would be 'The Taste Imagery'. People would bring their own lunches to eat. For a small charge they could order a paper mach'e copy of the food they really wanted that day. They could stare at it while they ate, and this would make it easier to imagine how the desired delicacies tasted.

We rolled on the floor imagining all the possibilities our imaginary restaurant offered. We even played the fantasy out, Marg being the waitress and myself the customer while holding my plum jam sandwich in my hand.

"Good morning."

"May I help you?"

"Sure, I would like to eat a piece of walnut cake and drink a cup of hot chocolate with whipping cream."

"Certainly," said Marg. She would place a Math book that represented the paper mach'e food sculpture in front of me.

"I hope you enjoy it!" I pretended to pay a forint, then started to eat my plum sandwich. After a few bites I would shout:

"Waitress! I am outraged! That hot chocolate model needs a new coat of paint. The whipping cream is peeling. I can't imagine the taste! Give me back my money!"

"Oh, I am sorry!" said Marg. "Really, the hot chocolate is quite worn. Please understand, it is in great demand. Dear lady, please don't ask for your money back. Would you like me to bring something else? The vanilla pudding is newly painted."

Marg and Sue have become grandmothers since then. They probably remember our high school years and 'The Taste Imagery' Restaurant with the same warmth that I do. Living in Hungary, they probably still line up while shopping for meat, but their selection of food is far greater than it was after the War.

Myself, I've been living for thirty some years in the West and I still have wonder in my heart. After all dreams do come true. When shopping at a supermarket and selecting whatever delicacy I want, I remember gratefully the little piece of orange peel. It taught me to appreciate what a blessed country like Canada can offer its citizens.

•••

CHAPTER X

•••

Not even 'hang man humour' could help to lighten the atmosphere in Hungary during the fifties. Many teenagers', short lives ended in those years.

Dorog is a coal mining village fifty kilometres from Budapest. The miners' barracks were built in rows on the gentle slopes of the Pilis Mountains. Everything seemed to be grey there, even the single family homes that lined the main street.

The centre of the villagers' social life was the community hall, called the 'House of Culture'. This was the place where I went twice a week for six years to teach ballet to three to fourteen year olds and folk dance to the fourteens and up.

Dorog was a place where people worked hard, and lived and died hard. To go hundreds of feet underground every day and risk your life requires desperate courage. The coal miners were called the 'Heroes of the Proletariate' and received better pay than other workers. They also got fancy uniforms and inspiring songs were written about them by others who never dared to go into the deep bowels of the black mines.

After finishing grade eight, many fourteen year old youngsters would go to miner school in the hope of making a few forint more than the rest. They earned more all right, but often spent it on hard liquor and so seldom got ahead. After a hard shift in the mine, the miners would sit in the pub and drink to wash the soot down their throats. Many miners even started the day by drinking schnapps taking two or three shots before they would go underground. Nobody cared about the drinking age. If people were old enough to work, they were old enough to drink. A mickey in the pocket became a symbol of manhood and of being strong and tough.

A young man named Jani had danced in my group for over three years. He had a small frame, dark skin and presented himself as being very confident. He spoke loudly, demanded attention, and bragged about everything he did or imagined he would do.

Jani often walked me to the train and sometimes even hopped on for the ride and the opportunity to talk longer. For that pleasure he had to take the long train ride back. That train took two hours to complete the fifty kilometre trip to the village.

I wish I had known more about human nature. Although I knew most of his talk was fantasy, at that time I was too young to see the desperation under Jani's confident mask. One night he lay down on the rails in the darkness and ended his dreams under the steel wheels of a train engine. His overcoat was folded neatly beside the track. He must have thought a good winter coat was too valuable to ruin along with his small body. With his coat he shed his mask of confidence leaving behind the broken body of what was a frightened eighteen year old boy who found life too dark, cold, and limiting for his dreams.

Jani's tragedy shook my heart with an iron fist. It taught me to look behind the roles people act out. Since then I have often heard desperation behind loud talk. Balanced and really confident people are rarely noisy.

Death was an everyday event in that coal mining community. Nobody made much of a fuss about it. All miners took their chances whenever they descended into the mine.

Miska was seventeen years old. After he had missed two or three dance practices, I finally asked: "Where is Miska? Why is he not here?" The dancers halted and gathered around the grand piano. Their answer came back: "Because he is dead!" I honestly thought they were kidding. A week later, Miska still hadn't shown up. "Come on kids, where is Miska? Did he quit the dance group?" I queried.

"Didn't we tell you last time that he is dead?" they replied.

"Yes, but I thought you were just joking."

"Oh, no," they said. "It's no joke. His remains were buried a few days ago. He was digging under a layer of burning coal which collapsed. All they could recover of him were a few bones."

I was shaken, but the young people looked at me as if I had a curious way of seeing life. "What is so tragic about that? It could happen to us any time. Today he is dead. Tomorrow we may be. Better to live it up until it happens!" They offered me a drink from their schnapps bottle and resumed dancing as though nothing had happened.

I came to accept their philosophy soon enough. One day in October 1956 - the month the Hungarian people rose up against the Communist government - I was walking along the torn streets of Budapest. Crowds of people were singing enthusiastically, crying from happiness, and hugging each other. We thought that the Revolution against Communism had been won, the Soviet had withdrawn and that Hungary was again free.

There were many corpses littered around. Many were Soviet soldiers, whose bodies had shrunk to the size of a three year old child in the excessive heat of burning tanks. Teenagers, fourteen to eighteen years old, had fought them with Molotov cocktails, so for every Soviet we had to bury a Hungarian, too. We put flowers on their bodies and prayed for them. We called them heroes and carried them to temporary graves in the churchyards. Life had become cheap and death seemed glorious. The excitement of the events swept me along with the others. We thought that the freedom of our country was more valuable than our lives.

Later when the Soviet tanks rolled over our newly gained confidence and freedom, I started to think about those days of glory with a shocking realization. I regretted the deaths not just of our own young people, but also of all the Soviet soldiers whose bodies had ended up on the blood soaked streets of Budapest. I was forced to think about their Mothers, sisters, and lovers who would be waiting for them to return. They had wasted their lives for a cause that had nothing to do with them. They did not believe in some higher mission. They had been used like mindless machines in the iron grip of the Soviet dictatorship.

In 1956 I was teaching in a factory where hundreds of young women were running textile machines. The dance group needed boys, too, so they had invited the A.V.H. soldiers to dance with them. The A.V.H. or State Defense Corps, was the 'strong arm' of the Communist State apparatus. They were hated by all civilians although the young men drafted into the A.V.H. from all over the country had no say when they were selected for this branch of the army. These draftees were chosen for their physical appearance. The A.V.H. needed the tall and the strong.

Young village men unwillingly trapped in A.V.H. uniforms came to dance happily. They were given two evenings off for practices. In dance groups these men could socialize with girls whereas the other soldiers often would not see members of the opposite sex for many months.

Two of the A.V.H. dancers - 'the Twins,' as I called them - must have been just nineteen years old. They were typical country boys: good, willing, and honest. They had heavy feet but listened to my instructions and tried their very best. The 1956 Revolution interrupted the dance class for several months. Afterward, when normal life resumed, 'the Twins' did not come to practice anymore. The rest of the young soldiers told me their story.

During the first days of the growing unrest, they were on duty controlling the demonstrating masses. The A.V.H. commander sensed that his troop was becoming increasingly sympathetic to the people of the city. Losing control over the situation caused the officer to panic and he ordered his troop to fire.

One of 'the Twins' refused. He just lowered his rifle beside his heavy boots and shook his head: "No." As others were hesitating too, the commanding officer shot the disobedient man on the spot. His 'twin' looked in disbelief on his brother's dead body, then turned his gun on the officer and killed him instantly. After that most of the troop joined the demonstrators or at least handed over their guns to help the crowd in the fight against the Soviet.

'The Twins'' story was a common one. All over Hungary, thousands of soldiers joined with the civilians. Firing on the people in that way turned the demonstrations into a Revolution.

The freedom of Hungary lasted only for a short time. The Soviet tanks rolled into the country and with them came the reinforced Communist government. They imprisoned or executed the disobedient soldiers and freedom fighters. Three hundred thousand Hungarians poured over the western border. Unfortunately, the second 'Twin' was not among them. He stayed behind to die.

•••
CHAPTER XI
•••

It took me four years to finish grades eleven and twelve because of difficulties I had with math, physics and chemistry. The importance of those subjects has been greatly over emphasized. They forcibly exercise only a student's left brain. Art was a much-neglected subject. The Communist regime did not need individualistic people who were creative and could think for themselves. They wanted followers - people who would obey the government and become part of the machinery that would work twelve hours a day.

Before World War II, the Hungarian economy was based on agriculture. The Communist government built hundreds of new factories in an effort to industrialize the country. They introduced three and five year economic plans. It was believed that the road to the future must be paved with realistic, down to earth school subjects. Math classes were held five days out of the six that made up the school week. Physics and chemistry took up the other five periods. Music or art was offered only once a week. Music meant singing and art only drawing. Being on correspondence, I did not have to take art at all. I studied subjects I did not have any interest in just so I would pass my final exams and get my high school certificate. To obtain this and be able to apply for university entrance, I also had to have high marks.

I studied without help, using the hours travelling to and from work. I read endless numbers of boring books. Mathematics was the greatest horror of all. I tried to solve the hundreds of problems presented in the thick text book without interest. My only motivation was the image of myself as a teacher in a high school surrounded by students. I visualized myself reaching out and helping them through their hard years of growing up.

I didn't care what subject I chose as a major as long as I could reach my goal. I preferred art, but it was a neglected subject in the curriculum, so I planned to become a history and literature teacher. Those two subjects seemed to reflect the struggles of mankind as well as the feelings of the individual.

I read numerous novels from the worlds classics along with the recommended Soviet contemporary writers who mainly painted a glorious picture of a Com-

munist heaven.

I wrote short stories and poetry myself. I put my feelings down on white pages and played with the enchanting rhymes of the poems. The paper accepted all my thoughts willingly, leaving my often heavy heart much lighter. I had tried to help people by listening to their problems; writing helped me much the same way. My thoughts became organized and my questions were answered.

Doing final exams was like going through torture. All examinations consisted of oral and written forms. The latter was by far the hardest for me. At the end of grade twelve I had to stand up in front of a committee, pull a question from a hat, and solve the problem on the spot.

Behind a long table were seated several teachers and the principal who looked at me like a judge in a courtroom. They were probably bored by the whole process and listened passively while the applicant read the question out loud with a shaky voice.

The history and the literature exams were easy. I just had to open the door to the storehouse of my years of reading. I could speak at length and enthusiastically discuss any novel or part of history in question. In fact, the examining committee had to stop my flood of speech.

It was much harder to stand up for math and physics. I had to solve the chosen problem on a blackboard and at the same time explain my procedure. Many years after this final exam I still had haunting dreams about standing there again, desperate, frightened, holding a piece of chalk in my shaking hand and trying to look confident. Only my dream to become a teacher got me through that.

Some thirty years later, I still wonder about the usefulness of some of the subject matter forced upon students. All the math I have had to do since high school graduation consists of adding up my expenses. Now we have calculators to do most of our math problems for us. For what did I suffer the horror of twelve years of math?

The school system and the curriculum have changed greatly since those days. The advantage of being creative and the importance of developing the right side of the brain are now acknowledged. Schools are finally taking the performing and visual arts seriously. However, the emphasis is still not equal. Art is just an elective, whereas mathematics is compulsory and comes first. Even if you want to be an artist, an actor, or a writer, to apply for university admittance, you must still have all the required, mostly left brained subjects.

When I finally obtained my high school diploma, I felt I had won a war. My good marks gave me the opportunity to apply to university and I took the entrance exams, but that was the closest I got to my dream at that time.

Every department in the university was overflowing with applicants. I wrote my entrance exams for the Faculty of Arts with a thousand other young men and women. We knew only the top ten to fifteen percent would make it. I was overwhelmed by happiness when, a few days later, I received an invitation to the oral exam. I was one of the lucky ones!

I remember walking all dressed up in my best clothes into the dark grey building of the Faculty of Arts on the banks of the Danube River. I felt immediately at home surrounded by walls breathing centuries of history and knowledge.

Twenty of us sat in a little hallway for hours, waiting to be called in. We wished each applicant well before he entered and excitedly questioned the one who had just completed the exam.

Finally it was my turn. In the rather small and narrow room, six people were sitting behind a long table. I glanced quickly at each of them. Their faces varied. The two professors looked distinguished and gentlemanly; the assistant professors appeared much younger but very friendly. Beside them sat a man in uniform and a woman in a cheap glaring dress. Both of them looked like hand picked examples of the state apparatus. They obviously represented the mighty Communist party.

I smiled toward them, hoping to look optimistic and confident, which I really was. As it turned out I was over-optimistic and over-confident.

One of the professors asked me some general questions, while the others asked more factual ones. Looking into the faces of the elderly gentlemen and seeing the intelligence and knowledge in their eyes helped me to formulate the right answers. At the end they shook my hand and expressed a desire to see me in their classes.

My spirit grew two little pink wings of happiness, and I gloriously flew out the door. Unfortunately I had paid little attention to the man in uniform and his partner. I spent the following week joyfully planning how I would manage to attend the university in the daytime while continuing to teach folk dancing in the evenings.

A week later, I got an other invitation to visit the faculty office. My positive mood lasted until I stepped through the door and found myself facing the same couple behind a large fancy desk. They did not ask me to sit down but just opened a folder of documents and asked:

"How many acres of land did your grandfather have?" I froze. My grandfather had died when I was five and I did not know the answer. They did.

"How many acres did your Mother have?" I knew the answer to this one, since the estate had only been lost in 1948 when all the privately owned land was swallowed up by the state farming project.

The last question was the cruellest. "What was your Father's occupation?" They knew it. It was recorded in the black folder, but they waited until I answered, feeling like I was admitting a crime: "Officer in the Hungarian Army."

I was always proud of my Father, whom I lost when I was only six years old. He died because his ideas and humanitarian thinking was far ahead of his time. He had been labelled a Communist because he stood up against the injustice of the old feudal regime. Entangled in a conspiracy, he was assassinated by another officer who envied him for his position. His story was wrapped up with the controversy and intrigue of sad human drama of World War II.

The man in the uniform looked at me with sarcasm. "Army Officer, eh? Supporting the Nazis against the glorious Soviet soldiers who brought freedom to our country? What does this mean? If you do not know yet, I will tell you! It means you are an enemy. Do you think the Communist government wants a teacher who belongs to the old regime? Your kind of people ruled long enough. Now the children of the working class are going to be the teachers. You should be grateful to work on an assembly line. You are dismissed."

I quickly left the office - my hopes lost and dreams fallen. I walked long hours beside the Danube before I was able to come to terms with my bitterness and anger. My story is not unique. It was quite common. I knew I had been harbouring an impossible dream. Despite the inevitable outcome, it hurt badly.

I was not alone with my feelings. The youth of Hungary had been pushed far enough, as had the farmers in the countryside and even the factory workers. The government had proudly stated that the proletariate now led the country while in reality, Stalin's red terror kept the government in power. Walking beside the

Danube, with my fists clenched in my pockets, I did not know the earth was already shaking underneath my feet. After all it was June of 1956.

•••

CHAPTER XII

•••

After the Soviet tanks had stamped out Hungary's short-lived freedom, thousands of people headed toward the western border. Families and friends parted from each other. Some decided to go; some could not pull up their roots.

I was ready to leave. I saw my chance to have a brighter future - opportunities to get my university education and rent a home all by myself. I was excited to think about a world where I would be able to speak freely and nobody had to fear jail just because their opinions differed from the ruling party.

Most Hungarians dreamed that America was a land of unlimited possibilities. We had a saying in Hungary for a person who got extremely lucky: "He found America." Most associated their fantasies of a utopian wonderland with the U.S.A. But it was not that way in my mind. I admired that giant, young and energetic nation, but my dream was to get to Canada.

I believed in the British parliamentary system. English law and democracy really appealed to me. I had heard that in Canada the government discouraged discrimination and every citizen had equal rights. The Kluh Klux Klan and the ghettos of the U.S. marred the ideals of what a country should be.

My great love of nature doubled my reasons for choosing Canada over the U.S.A. Canada to me was a land where people could find thousands of acres of wilderness, where forests grew and rivers flowed.

Although the border had been opened I had another hurdle to jump. This hurdle proved to be higher than my desire to go: I was in love.

One year before the October 1956 Revolution, I had met a charming young man who had enchanted me with his knowledge about almost anything we discussed. He was an assistant professor in the Faculty of Architecture, the son of two well-known teachers whom I greatly admired. We had dated for a year. I knew he was interested, but he had never told me he loved me or indicated any serious intentions.

I told him my plan to leave Hungary and met him for a final time. He looked at me with his huge dark eyes when I offered my hand for a farewell, then said the magic sentence: "Please do not go. I want to marry you." My legs got weak.

My heart jumped with joy and I stayed . . . stayed to face ten years of struggle to make a decent living, a home for us, and more hopeless efforts to get into the university.

We got married in the shadow of the Soviet tanks on the last day of 1956. Our wedding was very simple. We celebrated behind closed doors and drawn curtains. There was a curfew. After 9 P.M. anybody found out on the street was shot without question.

Still I was happy. Our love painted gold sparkles over the grim realities around us. Being married to the man I loved and carrying his son for nine months made those awful years which followed the Revolution some of the happiest of my life. I did not have to fear jail, as did so many others. After all besides cheering and crying with the crowd, I had only helped to put up barricades on the streets. In this act all citizens were equally guilty.

After the revolution my beloved new husband was fired from the university and had to accept a lower paid and less prestigious job in a government owned architectural firm. Planning projects was hardly his dream. There was a temporary cutback on folk dance groups, too. Consequently we had barely enough money to pay our portion of the rent for the apartment we shared with my Mother and the food bill for all of us.

A few years later we were financially a little better off, but our living standard was still far below what people in the west consider the poverty line. The magic of my son's birth kept me walking on clouds, but after some time the hardships overpowered the happiness.

My Mother had completely different ideas about child rearing from ours. Living together in a two bedroom apartment meant I had to respect her will. I was like a cushion between my mother and my husband, trying to please both and make our life as smooth as possible.

When I think back on my years between the ages of twenty and thirty, it seems obvious that I was not using my full potential in my teaching. I loved my students dearly. They then ranged from three years old to thirty, depending on which class they took - ballet, gymnastic, or folk dance. I was too pre-occupied with the glory of my youth and my motherhood and so did not devote my fullest attention to my pupils.

My ideas about changing the world for the better somehow had become secondary to my primary goal of improving my own life. I wished for nice clothes so I would look pretty, more money so we'd be able to afford to dine out or buy tickets for concerts and operas, and I also wanted to be able to have a few drinks in a bar if we felt like it.

The growing human being who was my son took a lot of my attention, too. The miracle of this child entrusted to me filled me with both joy and fear for his safety.

Until my son was born, I did not know fear. I had never been afraid for myself, but the fragile little fellow did not want to eat. He also cried a lot and woke me up some nights six to ten times. He was amazingly smart, he spoke like a professor in midget size, he started to walk because he wanted to get a book from the shelf. The possibility that some harm might come to him gripped my heart with iron fingers. I, who had loved everybody's children, felt such overwhelming love toward my own, it was almost too much to bear.

He was not interested in things most little boys do. He did not want to climb up on anything or kick a ball or get into little mischiefs. He was serious about this business called life. He declared time spent eating to be a waste and wanted us to read to him all the time. He spent his days looking at magazines and drawing pictures.

He was an only child constantly surrounded by older people. Consequently he learned to read before he went to school and talked with our friends using expressions he had picked up from my highly educated husband and his teacher grandparents. My father-in-law was like a great storehouse of information - a walking encyclopedia. He was retired and eager to teach his only grandson about the beauty of the academic world.

I sometimes felt silly sitting beside my son trying to trick him into children's play. One day when we were walking to his kindergarten, I saw a shiny long puddle that had frozen solid in the street. "Hey son, let's slide on it," I shouted and ran towards it happily sliding from one end to the other. My four year old carefully walked around the edge and shook his head in disapproval: "Little Mom, my little Mom, how can you be so childish?"

"What future is our little professor going to have?" I asked my husband one day. "What future are we going to have? Are we going to live forever without privacy? Will our parents tell us how to live until we retire? Shouldn't we make a change?"

After Stalin had died and the government's need to avenge the Revolution had pasted, life became better in general. People could express their opinions more freely. The Soviet Army still occupied Hungary and the one and only Communist Party still ruled, but the leading politicians had learned their lesson and 'pulled the cork from the bottle'. They had learned to let the bitter discontent spill over as a way to relieve the pressure so the anger would not explode again. They even issued some passports for people wishing to travel to the West. The numbers and time allowed were limited, but for the first time leaving became possible.

My husband and I applied. Our stated reason was that we wanted to take two weeks holiday in France. We waited for a half year. Finally the registered mail containing our passports to freedom arrived in 1965.

It was not an easy decision to make. It would mean leaving our parents, relatives, friends, and our jobs behind. The life that we had lived so long was very limited but relatively safe. Nevertheless we packed up a small suitcase. After all how much do you need for a two week holiday in July? Then we kissed all our loved ones for the last time. We could not know if we would ever see them again.

For me, the most painful moment came when I kissed the hand of my grandmother - she was in her eighties so there was little chance I would ever see her again - and looked at our collection of several thousand books. These were our only real material possessions, and I felt every volume was a personal friend.

Our son did not know he was saying goodbye to a life he had known only for seven years. He did not know he would be starting a new life in a few days on the other side of the Iron Curtain. My husband was thirty-nine and I myself was thirty when the train we had boarded in Budapest slowly crossed the Hungarian border and carried us toward a new and very different life.

●●●

CHAPTER XIII

●●●

My husband and I started our journey with $150 between us. That was the maximum currency allowed for those who wanted travel to the West, but it still was a great improvement over the Stalin era.

We gladly took that tiny amount which wasn't enough for a two-week holiday even with the most moderate and humble expenses. We did not plan to be tourists. We planned to start a new life. However, though we lacked money, we had plenty of determination.

My husband had an aunt in West Germany. This was the country we had selected as a stepping stone toward our real goal - Canada. We first set foot on the free land of the West in Stuttgart. There we checked into a modest hotel to sleep and the next day started our new life and the new day with optimism. First we visited Aunt Hedvig who some fifty years before had married a German gentleman and was living in a small three room apartment on a hill side.

My husband spoke German quite well. He belonged to the generation who had learned German in school and at home. When he was young, educated people learned a second language from childhood. Because I had grown up mainly after the War in a time when the Germans were considered Hungary's greatest enemies, I lacked skill in that language and was prevented from communicating. I sat politely smiling until my husband had explained our plans to our hosts over a cup of coffee and 'kuchen'.

Like many Hungarians, I had strong negative feelings toward Germans. The Nazi horror was part of my past. I had heard countless stories about their cruelty. I remembered the long lines of Jews being herded by soldiers toward an almost certain death. Many of my friends and students had lost parents and other relatives in the concentration camps. I thought about Julie, a young Jewish woman in the dance group, whose head and hand would shake out of control when she was under the slightest stress. She had numbers tattooed on her arm like a farm animal. Her heartbreaking story rang in my ears, while I observed the distinguished looking old person who was kindly offering us a helping hand to get established in the West.

The old couple had lost two sons in the War. As a result they were completely alone and hated the War that had robbed them of their children. They looked at my son with tears in their eyes and offered to have us stay with them in their home for a few months. They planned to go to an old age home soon and wanted to arrange everything to suit us.

We moved in the next day. While my husband almost instantly got a job in an architect's firm and started to earn money, I stayed at home cleaning the rooms, cooking and trying to be as helpful as possible. Two months later, we applied for a loan and bought the apartment and all the furniture and appliances that Aunt Hedvig and her husband did not want to take with them. In a very short time since we had stepped onto free land, we had a home and everything a person needs to lead a modest life.

After eight years of marriage we were finally alone. We had our own home! People born in the West can't imagine what that meant to us. It was a pleasure to vacuum the old oriental carpet and count the towels and hand embroidered bedsheets in the wardrobe. Each day I would open drawers and cupboards not really knowing what I was going to find. Even a year later I continued to discover new things - all of which belonged to us. I often cried from happiness and blessed the ground I walked on.

The German people were tremendously helpful and made us feel at home. I found them hard working and very disciplined.

Everything - every little chore of the daily life - made me happy. Going shopping was an adventure. After the long years of line ups for basic foods and consumer goods, I found that stores in Germany offered everything people behind the Iron Curtain could only dream about. Even the seasons did not limit the variety of vegetables and fruits. A weekday's shopping there was more luxurious than Christmas shopping in the old country. I could finally make an egg sandwich from three eggs all for myself without feeling guilty.

I signed up to take a language course, and within a year I felt confident enough to look for work. I visited the local employment office, and to my surprise, they found me a job. The gentleman who interviewed me apologized for not having an opening in dance teaching, but if I could . . . if I would be so kind to accept a job as a P.E. teacher in an intermediate school? He pointed out that my gymnastic background made me suitable. I hardly could believe in this miracle and quickly accepted the job.

My German was very limited. I bought a special dictionary dealing with sports terminology and wrote out long lists of words, posting them on the kitchen wall and repeating them endlessly while cooking or doing the dishes. My desire to teach overpowered the fear of dealing with a language I had not yet mastered. The administrators and my colleagues at the school were extremely helpful and tolerant. My grade five and six students were respectful, well-mannered and obedient. The gymnasium was superbly equipped even by North American standards.

I tried to make up for my limited vocabulary with body language when the word I was searching for did not want to surface in my overtaxed brain. While conducting a P.E. class, I used as much expressive movement as possible and led all the exercises by doing them with the students. Looking back at my two years as a P.E. teacher in Germany, I have to acknowledge my own bravery.

I felt the students responded well to me. My limited German even made my instruction more interesting to them. When my expressions made them giggle, I laughed with them and asked them to correct me. "I will teach you P.E. and you will teach me how to speak German," I told them. The ten and eleven year olds were proud to help me and I thanked them gratefully.

My different cultural background enriched the program. With creative dance, acrobatics, and gymnastics experience I was able to show the students new things. The games I invented made them laugh and jump with joy. They felt they were contributing to a new experience. The principal in the school gave me one instruction only, which I received with much relief: "Never line the students up. We do not want the P.E. class to resemble army training." The Germans had learned from the war after all. Living among them for three years, I shed all my prejudice. Average people are much the same on both sides of the Iron Curtain. They want to live their lives in peace and raise their children in hopes of a better future.

The horror of war and the extremes of party groups, whether green or red, Nazi or Communist, cannot be blamed on a whole nation. After all there were individuals in Hungary who had joined fascist terror groups in order to help to wipe out the Jews, and people with the same mentality had later become members of the A.V.H. with the power to torture and kill their fellow countrymen.

How had my seven year old son adjusted to our new home and new language?

He had finished grade one in Budapest, but upon arrival we re-enroled him in the first grade so he would repeat it in Germany. He was very small and fragile-looking. Though a year older he looked rather younger than the others in the class. On meeting my son the principal of the school shook his hand and then on a sudden impulse, leaned forward and kissed both his cheeks. With that warm, human gesture my previous nervousness disappeared.

The next day I had to drop my boy at the school ten minutes before eight. There were some thirty little German children lined up in the front of the closed classroom door. I held my son's hand and looked around, but there was no teacher in sight. Parents dropped their children off and left. The little people gathered together happily chatting with each other. My son looked at me and let my hand go. Saying: "Little Mom, do not worry. I will be just fine," he stepped into the group turning his back to me. I walked a few steps and looked back through my tears. His little body seemed so small and lonely compared to the well-developed German boys.

I learned the rest of the story from the teacher who had been sitting in another room, invisible to me and keeping an eye on the children. They had tried to talk to my son who did not understand them so he remained silent. The boys started to push him around, but still there was no response. They pushed harder and harder. The teacher had just stood up to go to his rescue when my son removed his glasses, put them safely into his school bag, moved the bag out of the way, and then jumped the biggest boy in the class. The unexpected move must have caught the boy off balance. He rolled to the floor while Jack gave him a few well placed blows. At that moment the teacher appeared. Everybody stood in silence. Jack collected his bag and felt a hand on his shoulder. Martin, another small boy with glasses, offered him his comradeship which lasted all through the three years we spent in Germany. The class accepted my son after what happened. Within a year he spoke German fluently, not just the 'hoch Deutsch' that the children learned in school, but the local Swabish dialect, too.

If you think that dealing with a new country, a new language, and a new job was a handful, I have to assure you that human performance has no limits. All you need is motivation. I was enthusiastic about this new life, about teaching and building a future for my children. Children, I say, because I had discovered I was pregnant. Nine months later I gave birth to a healthy, beautiful baby girl.

My daughter's arrival did not interrupt my teaching. I could afford to stay home, but being dedicated, after the three month maternity leave I was back at my job, part time. To the surprise of our neighbours in the apartment house (by this time they were all our friends), I would push the baby carriage three days a week across the road to the church day care. Half-time teacher and full-time mother, I enjoyed the best of both worlds.

At the end of our third year in Germany, our immigration application was accepted. The road to move to Canada was open. Let me tell you the truth. It was hard to leave Germany. There we had a good life, freedom and all the things that people born in the West take for granted. Immigrating meant we had to leave our jobs, liquidate our beloved home, and say goodbye to many friends. It was tempting to stay, but having talked the pros and cons over and over, we decided to follow our dreams and try life in Canada.

Remaining in Germany was still too close geographically to our pasts. There was the constant shadow of war. We feared that if the Soviet and American relationship deteriorated, our son might have to march as a German soldier against Hungarians who would have to support the Soviet. Having read about other countries' Constitutions, we were convinced Canada would be the best place to live. Thoughts of the vast land and the untouched wilderness there moved the teenage dreams inside me. I wanted to raise my children where lush forests cover the sides of the snow-capped mountains, where the blue Pacific meets rugged coast lines, where the grass is always green, and where we could afford a family home surrounded with a flower garden.

My husband and I packed our few suitcases and shortly afterward landed in Vancouver with a ten year old son and a ten month old daughter ready once again to start a new life in a new language.

PART 2

•••

CHAPTER XIV

•••

My story now leaves that landed immigrant family in 1968 to take a glimpse of the future some fifteen years later. My intention here is to put the spotlight on my efforts to reach my much-desired and much-loved teaching position.

Picture yourself in my 'clay room', where daily approximately 150 teenagers come to learn how to create objects from mud. The pottery wheels are turning. The tables are covered with spilled water, clay and muddy tools. My red labcoat is splattered and my hands which require constant washing are as red as my outfit. One of the students forgot to drain the tray around the wheel and the dirty water is now running across the floor and under the stools. The kids are laughing, talking, and mopping the floor. Some are even creating quite nice bowls and vases. Others are making trouble. One of the bright-eyed thirteen year olds has stopped my running between the tables and the sink to ask: "Hey, Ms. H! How many years did you have to study to get a rotten job like this?"

"Five years, my son," I answer. The kid shakes his head in wonder: "You must be crazy!"

He is right. I am crazy and I thank God for it. Everybody said the same thing when I signed up at the University of British Columbia ten months after my arrival in Canada: "Are you crazy? You do not speak English. You have hardly enough vocabulary to buy a loaf of bread at the store. How are you going to take university courses?"

Fortunately I did not listen. Bravely I turned up for the English Comprehension Test I was required to pass in order to gain admission. A friend had enlightened me about the nature of this exam. It involved writing a short essay on a chosen subject and completing a multiple choice questionnaire.

My English certainly was not good enough to write an essay on anything, so I had asked the same friend to write four one page essays on the likely topics such as "Why I came to Canada.

I have an excellent memory thanks to the endless Latin passages mastered in high school. I learned all four essays by heart.

Sure enough, one of the topics I had to choose from matched one I had memorized. All I had to do was to write it out neatly. I did alright spelling and all, for I have a visual memory and could see pictures of the words inside my head.

The multiple choice questions were harder. I read the sentences and had a vague idea about their meaning, but was not sure enough of selecting the right answer, so I closed my eyes and prayed for help: "Well God, here I am in the land of my dreams and at the doorway of my long-desired university education. I am thirty-four years old. I haven't too much time to waste. Please help me with the answers." Then trusting the higher power, I randomly marked what felt like the 'right' answers.

Miracles certainly happen. I got 68% on the test and was informed I could start my first year in September on the condition that I take an English course over the summer. That I did gladly. The higher a mountain is, the greater the challenge it is to climb. Motivation lies in the degree of difficulty of a task.

We had rented a modest little house. My husband had gotten a job as a draughtsman working for an architect. His diploma was not accepted right away. Unfortunately, this was hard on his ego for in Germany he had received full recognition right away. My son began 'New Canadian' classes and within three months we enroled him in a regular grade five, which he finished with a first class standing. My baby girl happily played with other toddlers at the house of an old lady who supplemented her pension with babysitting.

A year after our arrival we had melted into the multicultural fabric of Canadian society. I was grateful to have a home, a choice of life style, freedom of speech, and the opportunity to learn.

I can't remember who it was who advised me to major in P.E. at university, but I would like to thank that person now. She said: "You have taught folk dance, gymnastics, and ballet in Hungary as well as P.E. in Germany. This will be the easiest route to take. Besides, being a P.E. teacher will give you the best chance to get a job. They have the greatest turnover in most schools."

Taking that advice, this thirty-four year old mother of two started to learn the North American games and sports. I threw balls and caught them, ran miles on the track, hit a birdie with a badminton racquet, and dribbled basketballs across the gym floor.

"Tackling the impossible," is what many of my new friends called my university adventure. I aspired to do even more. My childhood love of drawing and painting finally found a practical outlet. When I had to choose another teaching area, I said firmly, "I want to teach art."

In school as a child I had been considered gifted in art, but those post-war years had made it impossible for me to develop my talent. In my youth I had attended many art history classes at the Faculty of Architecture, not as a student but just as an interested person. I was in love with the Italian Renaissance and admired all visual arts for their expression of human creativity. Also during our three year stay in Germany, we had travelled to Italy and France and had visited museums, cathedrals, and ruins from ancient classical times.

To study for university exams, I needed enthusiasm and determination. The dictionary became my constant companion. I took introductory English the first year and repeated it the second. I only tackled my first university level English course during my third year.

I had taken Latin for four years back in the old country. This helped me understand courses like Biology, Anatomy, and Psychology. Art History and Studio classes were a piece of cake compared with those. My P.E. classes kept me in excellent shape. Gaining weight was certainly not a problem. Our limited food budget ensured that, too. I found I had to cook as if I were back in post-war Hungary - cheap, basic food. My children did not suffer at all. They could eat fruit and vegetables year-round. Who needed other luxuries?

My son was occupied with his books and his studying. My daughter lived the life of a happy, healthy baby. Only my husband's life did not work out the way we had planned and hoped for. He was by then in his early forties - too late to adjust to the fact that he must start at the bottom again. He had begun his career in Hungary as an Assistant Professor. Now he was subjected to the uncertainty of his employer's financial success. I on the other hand was nine years younger than him and full of enthusiasm about my new life and university studies. We drifted apart.

Our story is a sad, human tragedy, not unique in any way, and it certainly does not fit with the purpose of this book. To make it short, he fell ill, developed terminal cancer, and died in the summer after my third year of university.

I hope you will forgive me if I stop for a minute to salute this noble, fine, very highly educated man who was the father of my children and my partner in life for fifteen years. He sacrificed his career to bring his children to a free land and to give them the opportunity to become whatever they would like to be. He helped me fulfil my dream of becoming a teacher. Without his understanding and support I would not have been able to reach my life's goal. I cherish his memory and I hope he can see me now - much wiser and much more patient with human weakness than I was at the time we had to say goodbye.

When we said goodbye to each other, he apologised for leaving me alone with the responsibility for two growing children. I apologised for not having given him full loving support for his struggle to cope with the hardships of our new life.

After his death, my friends expected me to quit university and take a 'real job' to support my children, instead of chasing an impossible dream. "Do you realize there are over three thousand certified teachers in B.C. without employment?" they asked. "Who is going to hire a P.E. teacher who is nearly forty years old and speaks only broken English?" one of them bluntly put it. "Nobody. You are wasting your time!" Yet I hung on to my dreams through it all. My children and I moved to a basement apartment on the east side of the city. I took all the loans I could get.

In 1973 I was called to the Citizenship Court. I read the oath through my tears and felt every word deep in my heart. Now my children and I were truly Canadians.

That same year in my cap and gown, I proudly accepted my Bachelor's degree.

However, with my degree I also received some shocking news. The twenty-one units I had completed in Fine Art would not make me eligible to teach art. The Faculty of Education would only accept six units. That meant I was twelve units short. My time was running out. Financially, it was almost impossible for me to spend more than one year in university, so I decided to take six units in the summer and six more in addition to the regular teacher training course load.

My sceptical friends spoke again: "What are you going to do with a Bachelor's degree? There is no way you will be able to pass the English exam you need to enter teacher training!"

I panicked: "What exam?" It turned out they were not just being pessimistic. The English exam was a reality. If you wanted to join to the force of the employable teachers in B.C., you had to demonstrate proficiency in English.

The thought of it brought me out in a cold sweat. German I had picked up within a year because I had heard it often enough in my childhood when Grandma and Mother talked those "Nicht for dem Kind" talks. During the war, radio broadcasts by the occupying Germans had added to its familiarity. Although I would have failed an exam in that language, too, I did then and still now do speak German well despite my heavy Hungarian accent.

I went home the night I learned of the exam to fix my family's usual cheap, budget dinner and then put my daughter to bed. I read her a bedtime story from her favourite book *The Princess and the Pea*, and sang to her while she slipped into peaceful dreams. I kissed her soft cheeks and wept.

There was my sweet little girl sleeping with her teddy bear, her toys scattered around a second hand bed and her room furnished with hand-painted furniture. Her future was entrusted to me. In the next room my son was studying long hours as usual. At the age of fourteen, he seemed to be the one in our family we knew would succeed. I never had to check that he was doing his homework. Quite the opposite - I often had to drag him away from his books and make him eat or sleep.

"Please God," I asked again. "Help me pass that English exam! Give me a miracle! I am a born teacher. I can't do anything else as well as I can communicate with young people. Do not let the past four years of painful effort studying English and writing exam after exam be a waste!" I was scheduled to appear a week later in the office of the head of the English Department in the Faculty of Education.

•••

CHAPTER XV

•••

That sunny morning in May 1973, I walked the cliffs at U.B.C. looking out over the breathtaking beauty of the blue sky, the snow capped mountains, and the deep azure ocean. Vancouver, the last paradise - that's how I felt about my new home.

My appointment with the English professor started at eleven A.M. After a sleepless night I stood on the edge of the cliff soaking the sunshine and the blue glory into my very soul. I thought to myself: "I am determined. I am devoted. I am confident about my ability to be an excellent teacher. I have two children to support and I am going to make it."

Tightening my fists, I put a positive, but not over-confident, smile on my face and knocked on the professor's office door.

"Good morning, come in, come in." A nice elderly lady rose from behind a large desk, walked toward me, and held out her hand. I shook her strong, warm hand and looked into her eye and saw a kind person who smiled and offered me a comfortable chair. She started to chat in a light conversational tone, as if we had been friends for a long time.

"Ah, you are Hungarian. I can tell that from your accent. It's very easy for me. I know Hungarians very well. I got my first teaching assignment forty years ago on the prairie in a little community where the entire village population spoke only Hungarian. Only the doctor and I spoke English. I had to teach the grade ones to read and write and speak English all at the same time. I was so young and so surprised by their way of life. You know, the women did all the work around the house. The men never helped. They sat on the porch drinking wine and smoking pipes. Are all the Hungarians like that?" she wondered.

"Oh, no," I answered. "Only the farmers. Educated people treat their wives as equals." I thought to myself: "I'm lying to her. Do I feel so ashamed of my own heritage? Could I not say the truth - that women's liberation had not gotten as far as Hungary yet? That it had been a huge task for the people to adjust to Communist ideas when the old feudalistic system had fallen apart?"

"When did you arrive in Canada?" she queried. "Are you married? Have you any children? Why do you want to teach?"

The questions followed one after the other. Her warm blue eyes put me at ease and I found myself able to talk to her, as if I were talking to a friend. But in the back of my mind I was still waiting for the examination.

"Oh you have a little girl! Do you read her bedtime stories? I adore fairy tales. You see I have several here even in my office." She took a book from the impressive bookshelf and passed it into my hands. "This is my favourite. Would you please read it for me?"

I opened up the book and read the title: *The Princess and the Pea.* Oh God, I thought, miracles do happen. I had read that story so many times to my daughter, I knew it by heart, so I imagined I was home and reading for my baby girl. I even acted out key lines. When I had finished and closed the book, a silence fell between us. "Next comes the exam," I thought.

The professor stood up. I remember she wore a pink wool dress. "Your 'Th"s and 'W"s are horrible. I advise you to take English 416. This is a speaking class, suitable for people who need to lecture. I teach it myself, so I will see you often. It was nice to meet you. Good luck!" She shook my hand warmly and escorted me to the door.

I can't remember if I thanked her or if I said anything at all. I stumbled through the door into the glorious sunlight, and while I walked among the flowering bushes planted around the old buildings I cried and cried from happiness. My professor has retired since then. I hope she is happy and healthy, but whether she is walking on the earth or in heaven, my blessings follow her everywhere.

The six units I took in the summer offered nothing but enjoyment. Exams? Who was afraid of them? Not me! My fifth year at the university was the best. I understood English and did not have to panic every time I answered a question incorrectly because of misinterpretation. All my subjects related directly to teaching. My fellow students were very helpful, and I also had a few master teachers to learn from.

The English Professor spent extra time with me after classes, and at the end of the year, she gave me a warm hug. "Beata," she said, "Your English is never going to be perfect, but you are going to be one hell of a good teacher."

I had the good fortune to have excellent role models at the university. Penny who taught fabric design and Michael of the art methods class were especially super teachers and the best human beings a person could ever encounter.

Penny became my role model later when I found myself running around in an awfully paint-spotted smock helping my own art students. Her unlimited energy, good humour, and genuine interest in people rubbed off on her students. Without her help and encouragement I would not have been able to finish teacher training or completed the missing units in art education within a year.

Since then, whenever I meet one of these rigid, humourless teachers who may mean well but do more harm than good for students, the examples of my English professor, Penny, and Michael remind me of the unlimited potential of the ideal teacher. Each year I have over 200 students entrusted to me to learn self-expression and human communication through Visual Art. Teaching them is a mighty task, believe me but I love the challenge. I keep my mentors' examples in front of me. Thus my success in teaching is their success, too. I repay them with my work trying to guide young people to be aware of their limitless potential and helping them to grow.

Despite all my hard work, at the end of my fifth year, in the summer of 1974, I still had to complete six more units of study. I was also short three weeks of required student teaching time. I was determined to get a job in September regardless. My friends again warned me: "You are crazy! Who is going to hire you without a Professional Certificate when all the school boards are flooded with applications from highly qualified teachers?"

That was the reality, all right, but again I tried to tackle the impossible. At the beginning of June I set out job hunting. I applied to every school board in and around Vancouver. I did not mention the fact that my certification was not complete. I just could not afford to wait another year.

Disappointed, I never got even one interview. Somebody told me that it was useless because the school boards were filing all applications without even looking at them. I did not know if this was true or not, but I just could not sit back and wait. I opened up the phone book and wrote down the addresses of twenty-five schools. After that I dressed up as smartly as I could and set out on a school-to-school job search.

Starting with the closest address, I did always the same. I would walk in and introduce myself to the secretaries. With a polite, but firm manner, I would ask to see the principal. Sooner or later, I got through the principal's door. I would repeat my introduction and say, "I am looking for a teaching position. I am a new Canadian, thirty-nine years old, widowed, and a mother of two. My subjects are Art and Physical Education. I am a devoted teacher with European experience. If you are interested in having a good teacher on your staff, I will be more than happy to work in this school."

None of them laughed in my face. All of them listened politely. They expressed how sorry they were, but that they had just hired somebody or they did not need anybody. All of them wished me good luck, and I think they meant it, too.

After visiting the second school I completely lost all nervousness. The atmosphere of the schools - the smell of the hallways - made me feel like I was going home. I just had to find the right door.

The eleventh school was the one. I felt it right away. Following a sketchy map, I got lost on the way there. The school was outside the city in an area surrounded by bush and with only a few new homes and long stretches of empty streets. The principal asked me many questions. Fortunately none of them pertained to my certificate. He told me he did need someone because one of the P.E. teachers was going on a leave of absence. He would phone when he had decided.

When I left his office, I saw two other applicants waiting, both of whom were much younger than I was. Probably their documentation was in perfect order as well. In spite of that, I still felt optimistic.

It took me a long time to find my way home. Just as I reached my front door, I heard the phone ringing. With a shaking hand I turned the key and ran to pick up the receiver. Just as I had expected, it was the principal phoning to let me know I was hired. I was in seventh heaven. I had made it! I had a teaching position. To describe my happiness exceeds the capacity of any written words. The next day I was to go back to the school to see the facilities and meet my future colleagues. I loved everything about the school and could hardly wait 'til September.

But first I had to attend summer school and then make up the missing student teacher training. I had no idea how I'd do that and be a teacher at the same time? How many more impossible hurdles would I have to jump?

•••

CHAPTER XVI

•••

Early that summer I received a phone call from the school board where I'd been hired. "Do you know you are not going to get your professional certificate this summer?" Did I know it? "God!" I thought. The lady who phoned asked another pointed question: "Do you know that in B.C. there are three thousand teachers who are seeking employment? Their papers are in perfect order. The school board can select any of those highly qualified people!"

"I realize this, but I am in desperate need of a job. Please make an appointment for me with the Superintendent," I replied. She was kind enough to do that.

Again I was to take on the impossible. I drove to the school board office with butterflies in my stomach, hands shaking, and wild ideas running through my mind regarding how to convince the Superintendent to hire me instead of those highly qualified others. "Please God help me!" I pleaded. "Guide me while I am presenting my case!"

The Superintendent looked like a real gentleman. He was handsome, too. That made me feel better. I took a seat in front of his huge desk and tried to look confident and calm.

He asked basically the same questions as the secretary on the phone. He pulled my job application form from what must have been a bottomless filing cabinet. He pointed out the missing data and looked at me questioningly. What did I have to loose? I took a deep breath and just said what was in my heart. "I am a teacher, not because the U.B.C. papers say I am, but because of my inner feelings. I am devoted to this profession. I know my certification is not in order yet, but I can't wait any longer for a job. I am thirty-nine years old. My daughter is six; my son is sixteen. I started life in Canada from scratch six years ago. I need to work. If I get that teaching appointment, it will be a lifetime commitment on my part. I will do a very good job!"

I talked about my dance-teaching career in Hungary and about my two years teaching P.E. in Germany. By hiring me, the school board would gain not just another teacher, but somebody who knows a lot about life, people and hardship, and above everything else has limitless love toward teenagers.

When I finished, he smiled. I knew I had won. When we shook hands it felt like I had made him a commitment to live up to my promises. Well, I did. I have stuck to my word and kept that teaching job through good and bad, doing my very best always.

I received a letter of permission to teach, and in September I began as a P.E. teacher replacing the lady who had gone on her leave of absence. In October I was called to complete my three weeks of student teaching in a North Vancouver high school. I wonder if it has ever happened to anyone else - being a student teacher while you are already a teacher?

I fell in love with art education while at U.B.C. My student teaching just reinforced this feeling. Art is one of the most important tools you can use to motivate people toward creativity and inventiveness. It is a subject that teaches children to think, not just memorize facts. As well, art classes teach students to be themselves and express their unique individuality through a variety of media. Art teachers have the opportunity to get close to every student in the class to know their personalities, their problems, their hopes, and their dreams. What a magical world!

Even with all the enthusiasm I had toward teaching, I did have some problems with the Canadian physical education system. Competitive sports make up the major part of the program. Basketball, hockey, and volleyball classes were not the ideal setting for me to convey my kind of educational philosophy. Standing beside the playing field and blowing a whistle to enforce rules was harder than I had ever imagined.

For one thing the customary way of selecting teams always made my heart sink. The confident, talented girls invariably organized their teams with the aim of winning. The team captains would first choose the fastest, most skilful girls or their best friends, leaving the overweight, the unskilled, the shy, and the lonely types until the last. When the teacher finally assigned them to the teams, the other students would openly express their displeasure: "How can we win? She'll just drag our team down?"

Why is there always such an emphasis on winning? Why do we condition our students towards winning? Aren't having fun and learning new skills just as important? I often tried to explain that to my students without much success. They were born and raised in a competitive society, which always divided the winners from the losers.

To prevent unhappy scenes I gave the unwanted other chores. I invented various important tasks for them like keeping the score or collecting and counting the balls and rackets. I tried to make them feel necessary and wanted.

Fortunately, the school had only one gymnasium. It was generally occupied by the senior P.E. teachers. I had to teach outside on the field, or when the weather turned rainy and cold, I used the cafeteria or an empty classroom. I took this golden opportunity to revise the P.E. program.

I carried a cassette player and had the students warm up to music. I taught the girls to move with the beat first with their feet, then with their hands, finally using their whole bodies. I started units on dancing, teaching folk, jazz, and creative dance. I gave the girls balls, hoops, and ribbons to use creatively. I had them explore how many different ways they could throw and catch, move with the hoop, jump a rope, and so forth.

Most of the girls who had been the stars in basketball or soccer proved to be heavy and slow moving when it came to dance. The previously unwanted girls started to excel. They figured out more creative ways to use a ball than anybody else. Most of them had a good sense of rhythm and moved gracefully. I asked what kind of interests they pursued after school. It often turned out that they played the piano, took ballet lessons, or wrote poetry.

The P.E. department head was not pleased with my way of conducting these classes. He was shocked when he stepped in the room and saw me dancing the twist with thirty girls shaking their bums in shorts. He almost fainted when another time he found the same group sitting in the lotus position silently practising yoga breathing. P.E. department meetings often ended in polite but heated disagreements between my ideas and the goals of the department. When it came to coaching I chose to sponsor the gymnastics team. That was the safest ground for me.

My experiences with P.E. teaching awakened a lot of thoughts in me. It became obvious to me that students have a great variety of individual interests and skills. In Canada we have unlimited space - for example a green field around every school - and should be able to accommodate a variety of different programs.

In Europe, due to the lack of space, P.E. was always confined inside. This resulted in the P.E. program beneficially favouring dance and gymnastics. Why can't we use the green spaces around our schools for less competitive, fun games and add breathing exercises and individualized programs like tai chi to the program? Do the girls really need to run as much as we force them to? The physical structure of the female body does not have the same developmental needs as a male body. Most of the girls in school hate running. I can relate to that. With all the skill and stamina I gained in dancing, I would faint if I had to run around the track. I know; I tried it. As a result, I let my students choose if they wanted to run or walk without being timed.

I do see the importance of athletic competition. It gives certain individuals an opportunity to stretch their physical potential to greater heights. Competitive sports give the physically gifted a chance to perform. But, is it right to base our whole school P.E. program on the competitive spirit? Strength, fitness, and endurance are great qualities, but some students have to exercise their minds and feelings more than their bodies. As in Visual Art, schools could offer programs in which individual differences can easily be accommodated. Physical self-expression should be the aim of the P.E. curriculum.

To individualize the P.E. program would require more work from the teachers. It is much easier just to stand beside the field and blow a whistle. I seriously considered devoting myself to reevaluating P.E. classes, but being new to the school, new to the Canadian school system, as well as having only a temporary appointment and a limited English vocabulary, I did not have enough status or security to pursue the issue.

Every time I had a spare or some free time, I visited the art room. Jutta, a petite energetic lady with warmth in her heart, spent lots of time with me talking about everything I was interested in knowing. We became friends. She was not just a teacher, but an artist, too. I expressed my desire to teach art and she helped me get acquainted with the art teacher's world. Compared with the limitations of the Physical Education program, the Visual Arts offered unlimited potential to individualize my teaching. I knew this was the place for me!

The following year the teacher whom I had replaced came back to her job. Because of the growing population of the area, I was kept on anyway, teaching half time P.E. and half time Art.

The goddess of fortune kept me in her parlour. My Professional Certificate was issued and in the fall of 1975, I put a smock on over my track suit and faced my first art classes. Throughout the second year, Jutta gave me a helping hand.

Toward the end of that year she announced her plan to quit and move to the North which left me in the position to teach full time art. If this is not a success story, then what is?

For me success meant not just acquiring the position I wanted after so many years of hard work. What meant the most to me was the response of my students to the way I handled them.

Two years after my P.E. teaching career was over, an ex-student, Debbie, visited me. She had become such a pretty young lady, I found it hard to recognize her as the same girl who had carried the P.E. equipment and sat beside me jotting down the scores. She was then overweight and hid her bad complexion under a mop of hair. She smiled brightly and said: "I came here to thank you for giving me confidence in myself. You told me I am worthy and beautiful. You even gave me a good mark in P.E. and made me your assistant. You saved me from being the scapegoat of the others. Do you remember? You told me I can be whatever I want to be. All I need to do is believe in myself strongly enough and try. I wanted to be slim so I quit eating junk food and took dance lessons. I slimmed down within a year. I used to eat bags full of potato chips and many chocolate bars because I was frustrated. I needed a way to comfort myself when everybody was hurting me. Nobody laughs at me anymore. You saw the better me inside and inspired me to bring it out. Thank you." My adventure teaching P.E. was not without value after all.

•••

CHAPTER XVII

•••

When I was fifteen, I promised myself I would never forget my own difficult teenage years. I have kept my promise and my memories of all the years of struggle to make a living and raise my children are still fresh.

It is surprising how many adults forget their own adolescence and how they felt then. Most grown ups can't relate to teens. Parents are completely stunned when their sweet little children suddenly begin experimenting with alcohol, smoking and sex - all very much a part of the adult's world.

Young people rebel against rules. The more their parents try to enforce them, the more their children resist. This creates constant conflict. On one side are the parents who want to save their teens from making the same mistakes they did; on the other one the young and curious who want to try everything that was forbidden them in childhood.

It is so easy to love an innocent child with sweet curls and a soft little face who cuddles up to you and looks up to you like you look up to God. Mom kisses little hurts better. Mom and Dad know everything and take care of all the infant's needs. In the eyes of the young child, parents are God-like creatures. The child trusts them and loves them without reservation. As the child grows up, he suddenly realizes his Mother and Father are just like other human beings. Parental glory fades, and the teenager bitterly blames his Mom and Dad for not being any better than other adults. The next step is to start questioning their authority, their values, and their judgements. The teen asks uncomfortable questions and talks back loudly to express his disappointment because his parents are not perfect. The parents seem like Gods fallen from the sky of childhood adoration.

How many of you have thought back, perhaps only fifteen or twenty years, to the time you went through all this? Very few of us do, unfortunately. Even if you remember, you think: "My adolescence was different. I did a better job with my children than my parents did with me."

Most adults have the same misconceptions about their children: "My daughter or my son will never do all those awful things. There is no way my child will experiment with sex at an early age or drink alcohol before the legal age. Other teenagers yes, but not my own! I raised my child teaching strong values." If the parents are the fallen gods, the children become the fallen angels. On both sides, disappointment arises because of unrealistic expectations.

Of course, some young people do study hard and lead a life which pleases their parents. They don't smoke, don't drink, and bring home top marks. They are in the minority, I would say. Much of the growing generation takes shorter or longer trips on the 'wild side'. Sometimes they are able to keep their explorations secret, if the parents are so 'love-blind' that they don't notice what their youngsters are up to. The more rebellious spirits start to show openly that they control their own lives and will do exactly the opposite of what is expected of them.

In my experience the so-called rebellious teenagers - the troubled ones - have the most interesting personalities. They are not willing to copy their parents' ways. They are questioning and re-evaluating everything. I have found many bright and unique personalities hidden behind unruly acts. Such children feel that they can't obtain guidance from traditional ideas. Religion failed as a guide for most youngsters a long time ago. The fear of God and eternal hell might have worked centuries ago, but it certainly won't keep today's youth in line.

During my childhood, parents disciplined us with spankings at home and at school. But I wonder what is the use of good behaviour if it is performed only because of fear and not in the light of true knowledge of right and wrong? Eye opening experiences and life's lessons - these do more to guide a person's actions than any fear of authority.

Taking a walk on the wild side can be very beneficial. Bad experiences can be the best deterrent. They teach a young one more than any preaching coming from parents, teachers, or ministers. When you fall down, you have to pick yourself up and learn to walk to avoid further disasters.

Never doing anything bad does not necessarily make you a good person. Most of us are familiar with those uncaring, unloving individuals, who sit on a pedestal of high morals. They are never wrong; they're always right; and from their cold iron seat of unquestionable values, they judge everyone. They have no sympathy for human weakness and look upon their fellow human beings as sinners. In my opinion, these people do more harm to mankind than criminals who are behind bars. Whether they are parents, political leaders, priests or teachers, if put in charge of other human beings they become dangerous. God save young ones from a teacher who never makes a mistake and who knows it all. In my youth, when students never even dreamed of talking back, adults had unlimited power to kill budding human spirits and discourage youngsters from ever being themselves.

If the general student body hates a teacher, there is a good reason to suspect that person is in the wrong profession. Probably he or she is a bad teacher. Our public education system has a lot of room for improvement, but we can be proud of the fact that students now are not afraid to tell a teacher their opposing views.

Relating to the problems of teenagers and understanding their follies are easier if you remember going through all this yourself. The best drug rehabilitation programs are run by people who were once drug addicts. If we want to reach convicts and retrain them to be valuable members of our society, we'd better start to hire ex-convicts to run the re-educating programs. "I know what you are going through. I have been there myself" works. Most troubled teenagers are looking for affection and somebody who understands and cares. Those who are acting up the most are the most in need of love.

The B.C. school in which I was first hired had more than the average share of 'bad' kids. The area, being a long way east of Vancouver, offered relatively cheap housing. Low income families could afford to rent or buy a home there. The police made daily appearances in the school, and there were days when we had anywhere from three to six false fire alarms. The students favoured the fashion of the 70's: fringed jeans, torn and faded jackets. They carried jackknives and cigarettes in their pockets. A class of thirty to forty kids was not pretty to look at. It was 'cool' to look tough, but I loved them. Facing a class of thirteen to fifteen year olds and trying to teach them gave my days meaning and challenge.

At the beginning of the year the toughest ones would try to push me around to see how easily I could be manipulated. Coming late to the class was the first thing they tried. When they would open their mouths to say some excuse, I would beat them to it and jokingly list all the usual possibilities: "My locker got stuck. I felt sick in the bathroom. Another teacher stopped me in the hallway." I said all this with a twinkle in my eye - smiling away the tension and finishing the list with such excuses as: "I did not want to waste my cigarette. I curled my hair and put on my make up, because I can't do it at home since my Mom thinks I'm too young." The students would look at me in surprise expecting a detention.

Instead I would ask them to be honest. "Tell me the truth all the time. Do not use lies. I know more excuses than you can ever dream up. Come in time for the explanation of the class work. When everybody knows what today's class is all about, if you have the urge to smoke, you may leave." They did not believe their ears. Later one of the leaders - a brave student - stood up. "May I go to the washroom now? I really need a cigarette!" "Of course," I said. "You have five minutes. That's enough. I know because I smoke myself."

Surprisingly enough, they did not take advantage of this 'washroom privilege'. Smoking in the school of course was forbidden. Going to the washroom to have a cigarette was against the rules. Because I took the fun out of it, I am sure fewer students left my classes during the period and rarely did they arrive late. As one of the younger ones put it: "I wanted to bug you Ms. H., but then I figured you are cool, so I stopped."

I can feel some of my readers' reactions to the above story: "What kind of teacher is she encouraging smoking?" It's shocking, isn't it? My leniency toward smoking shocked the students, too. Being caught smoking meant suspension, but they did not hide their cigarettes when I stepped into the washroom, and they did stop lying to me. They knew I was never going to report them.

Did they fear the punishment? Not at all. They smoked to get attention, not because they really needed a cigarette. Caught for smoking they got what they had been asking for all along. I heard countless times the proud statement: "I got kicked out because of smoking." The less adventurous students looked up to these rebels admiringly and they felt like heros. "I'm cool, I smoke. I'm not afraid of the vice principal. I'll laugh if I'm suspended." Just think back, dear parent. If you ever smoked why did you start it? What was the original impulse that drove you to light up your first cigarette? Be honest with yourself.

I remember my first cigarette at the late age of seventeen. (I grew up with the limitations of the post-war era, remember?) I was a married woman and a dance teacher, so of course I had to enhance my dramatic new image by lighting those stinky, strong, no filter cigarettes. I liked my independent, self-sufficient self, and cigarette smoking was part of it. Smoking seemed to mark my entrance into the world of adults. But I also got hooked. Later on, the more trouble I faced in life, the more I smoked. I stopped during pregnancy and childbirth, but after those intervals I always restarted. It was easy to find excuses for it. Problems came by the hundreds throughout my adventurous life.

I continued to smoke until I developed chronic bronchitis and my constant coughing interrupted my teaching. That forced me to think: "Do I want to die or do I want to accomplish more in life?" Then I put down my last cigarette and have never picked one up since.

My struggle with smoking amplified my will to try to save young people from getting hooked on cigarettes, but I knew if I preached at them, it wouldn't work. It would not even work for me to be a role model myself. Instead, if I showed an understanding of their bad habit and won their trust, it might be possible to tell them my opinions about the subject without having my message fall on deaf ears.

I would tell my students how I started to smoke, why I did it and how much I enjoyed cigarettes which hurt my health after all. My students would look at me in horror when I went into my coughing fits. Then I would say, "It's better if you don't smoke. The longer you do, the harder it is to kick the habit." "If you still want to kill yourself, it is your privilege," I would add, "But it would be a shame if you develop lung problems like I have" or "You're young, good looking, and have your whole life ahead of you. Are you going to miss out on a lot and end up wasting away because of a stupid cigarette like I did?"

When my friends and fellow teachers organized a stop-smoking clinic, I signed up and brought dozens of students with me. "Ms. H. wants to quit smoking," they told each other, "I'm going to try it, too." Some of them smoked a few cigarettes before we went in, just to show off in front of their peers, but they all acted like hard core hooked on drug addicts and came to the smoke clinic.

My teacher friend, Jerry, who was fifteen years younger than I was and a heavy smoker, had tried to quit for the last two years. He was a living example of the old joke: "It's easy to quit; I've done it hundreds of times." However, caring for his students like I did for mine and being too weak to resist the temptation of a good cigarette alone, we teamed up against our own bad habit and especially against the hazard that cigarettes represent for the young and inexperienced.

We won. Both of us eventually quit for good. Many of our students re-evaluated the value of smoking in light of our triumph. They understood smoking is, after all, a killer and that it is not worth risking your health for the sake of looking 'cool'.

Nowadays smoking is not such a big problem. The awareness of the cigarette hazard has increased to the degree that smoking in public places is forbidden. Also, cigarettes have become so expensive it is hard to buy them on a student's budget. Only a very small percentage of our students still smoke. This is no longer the major problem it was in the 1970's. If, dropping into the student smoke pit, I find an occasional smoker, I bring back my old tricks that worked so well in the past: "Don't worry, I won't report you. I understand. I went through it myself. No, I'm not mad at you at all. I feel sorry for you. You're such a good looking young person . . ."

I call it a trick, but the message is true. The words come from my heart, for I do understand teenagers when they light up. How about you? . . If your answer to this question is "No," you probably have little chance of saving your children from smoking.

•••
CHAPTER XVIII
•••

When I moved to Vancouver I was amazed by its mixed population. Taking a bus through the city or walking on the streets seemed to be an exotic adventure.

During the late 60's and early 70's, the Kitsilano area was still the centre of the flower children. I had never heard about hippies before I came here, and it surprised me to see young mothers walking the sidewalks bare foot, dressed in flowing gowns, flowers in their hair, and carrying babies. Young men with long hair strolled along carelessly, obviously with no burning desire to work. This was a brand new concept for me - somebody who does not have a job and is still able to eat and go on with his life. In Europe people worked just to stay alive. The hippies in Vancouver doing nothing but having fun managed a better standard of living then many who worked all their lives in the old country.

Listening to their life philosophy shook up old desires from my teen years: "Get back to nature. Live in the Wilderness. Make love, not war." At that time, however, my day consisted of taking my daughter on the early bus to her baby sitter and carrying heavy books under my arm as I ran from class to class at U.B.C. In the afternoon I would shop for food, clean, cook, and play with my children. When they went to bed, I would study half the night. I did all this without bitterness for I wanted to reach my goal. My heart was filled with gratitude for my new country that had provided me with the opportunity to reach my goals in life.

It was at U.B.C. that I first heard about the drug problem. Smoking marijuana seemed to become popular with the hippy movement and remained fashionable throughout the 1970's.

It took me a while to comprehend the problem. In the old country the only drug I had ever encountered with was alcohol. People there drank to forget poverty or to have a good time. They drank to celebrate and to mourn. Smoking marijuana or using hard drugs was unheard of.

When offered marijuana, I looked at the green dry weed with distrust. I wondered what it could do to me. I tried it out of curiosity and found it uninteresting. It smelled too sweet, tasted too sweet, and did not make me feel high. Probably the short drinks that the coal miners had shared with me in my early youth had made me immune. In short, I did not find any enjoyment in it and had no desire to explore it further; however, this experience came in handy when I started to work with teenagers. Marijuana seemed glamorous to the teenage students of the 1970's. It was exciting because it was forbidden.

At the beginning of the year, I would have my students make art folders with a personal logo for identification. "Draw a design for your folder a picture of something you associate with or are interested in and that expresses you as a person."

This first project had the result of mapping out the class for me - dividing the grade eights into groups with common interests. The sweet little girls still close to childhood would draw rainbows, flowers, butterflies and unicorns. The boys would mainly use sport symbols or pictures of expensive cars. A few who were trying to look grown up and cool would draw beer and whisky labels. That would leave a small, but noticeable, group who drew skulls and marijuana leaves.

I would never object for I was the one who had told them to label their art folders with the symbols they were most interested in. The students would look at me with some uncertainty as I walked behind them and looked over their shoulders while they drew. I probably disappointed their expectations by not showing any shocked expression. I would calmly comment about the shapes and the colours, but would make no further remarks.

This project gave me a good overview of the class right from the start. The rainbow, flower, and car drawing students would be easy to handle - at least for the time being. The beer label and the marijuana drawers tended to need most of my attention. There lay the challenge and opportunity to provide guidance.

The folder design also helped me discover hidden talents in terms of artistic skill and individual spirit. One quiet, blond boy's logo stopped me for a while. The background of his large paper envelope was covered with shadow-like heads turned toward each other as if they were gossiping together. In the foreground, there stood out a lonely boy's profile coloured blue. "What is your name, son?" I asked. "Ron," he whispered shyly. "I think your design is very interesting." "Do you like it, Ms. H.?" "Yes, I do. Please tell me what title you would give to this picture?" Ron looked at me with clear intelligent eyes. "Being different," he said simply.

The marijuana folders had to be hidden when the principal strolled in to view the art class. It would have been too hard to explain why I had let the students draw such designs. This particular principal had no feelings for art himself. He was there to enforce the rules. Any possible explanation like: "Art is self-expression" would not have impressed him. He was disliked by students and teachers. I think he had good intentions, but did not know how to deal with people. With his effort to control the staff and students, he generated hatred. His presence did not make the teachers' tasks any easier.

Keeping in mind what I had learned about my students from their first drawings, I started to deal with those who needed guidance. It took some extra effort at the beginning of the year to get to know all the students individually. By 'knowing' I don't mean just learning their names. Having on average 200 students in seven classes, that was not an easy task in itself. Still emphasizing the need for artistic freedom of expression and encouraging each to draw his own way helped me to accomplish my aim.

Besides the regular art projects, like object or nature drawing, I gave my classes assignments to help them open up. "Draw your own face from a picture, from a mirror, or from memory, or instead, draw yourself as you feel inside." The finished projects revealed a lot about the students' personalities. Half of them choose the "feel inside" portrait. A shadow picture of a head with question marks in it, tangled lines expressing confusion, broken hearts, tears for pain and disappointments, a small human figure in the corner of a dark fearful forest - these are only a few of the symbols I considered important. Very few of the kids used bright colours or drew balloons or flowers for happiness. The thirteen to sixteen year old's life is not something we can envy. Very few of them have direction or confidence or enjoy life.

The same teenagers who tended to draw marijuana plants, also made dope pipes from clay when the pottery unit started. I do not think they ever wanted to use them, but it was a great way to show off. My resisting this would have blocked the communication. You have to build a bridge between two points in order to get across. Helping them calmly with their work gave me an excellent opportunity to start conversations on the subject of drugs.

I learned from them who was smoking dope, where they got it, and why they did it. Most of them were motivated by the thrill of doing something illegal. Shocking adults with their behaviour was fun and it served a multiple purpose. They would draw adults' attention to themselves and at the same time they could play the big shot in the eyes of their peers.

We carried on several informal conversations about the subject. "Do you smoke marijuana, Ms. H?" they asked. "No, but I tried it. It didn't do anything for me." I spoke to them truthfully. "Furthermore, I have read about drugs extensively, and I figure drug use does not pay off in the long run." I stopped there and waited until they nagged me for more information. "Well you know, marijuana might make you feel good and help you to forget problems, but there is a big price to be paid and I do not mean money."

"What big price?" they persisted.

"It kills your brain cells."

"So what!" they laughed. "I don't have much of a brain to start with," one of the boys declared.

"You have a low opinion of yourself," I told him.

"Well, I'm failing in almost everything."

"Oh, that may be what you have chosen, but you can't trick me. I know you're smart. I've observed you. You're bright and intelligent. You could have A's in your other subjects if you wanted to, but you hide your brain. You think it's cool to fail."

The boy looked at me in surprise. "How do you know I have brain?"

"I've seen your drawings. They give you away. You are smarter than you give yourself credit for. It's a shame you're killing your excellent brain with that dumb weed."

Another casual conversation had a different end. Boys and girls that age think about sex more than their parents can imagine. "Well, if you'd rather smoke dope than have a love life when you grow up, that's your choice," I said.

"What does it have to do with your love life?" I could tell from the brightness in their eyes they were paying attention.

"You see, marijuana makes you impotent. If you smoke regularly, you eventually will not be able to make love."

"Are you sure, Ms. H?"

"Yes, you can bet on it. I have read about drug use in depth and I have a friend who got impotent from dope. Even ladies lose their interest in sex, not just men."

I was stretching the truth by inventing a friend and reading extensively on the subject in a good cause. I wanted to scare them off drug use. It worked. Many of my students decided smoking dope was not worth the risk. "Ms. H. said it. She knows. She smoked herself. She has a friend . . ." No amount of preaching or formal lecturing would have achieved the same result in those years.

Now it is easier at my school. The population of the area has changed greatly and the general spirit of the student body has changed with it. By the end of the 1980's, the well-dressed teenagers walking the halls resembled a fashion show. High heels replaced dirty runners full of holes. Swirling skirts and expensive tops replaced short cut T-shirts and fringed jeans. The students now don't light up marijuana cigarettes to create excitement. Still behind the well-groomed appearance, the kids are the same love and attention seekers. The outward form has changed, not the inner substance.

Ron, the shy blond boy I mentioned before, remained 'different' throughout his high school years. At one point he dyed his hair electric blue. For months I had to hide him in the art room during lunch or after school to avoid confrontations with the tougher boys. He had eccentric ideas and a great talent in art, and we remained friends throughout the years even after he graduated. Currently he makes his living as a professional artist, exhibiting in Toronto, New York and Paris. His success did not make him forget me, however. Recently he phoned long distance and told me about his hopes and dreams.

The lonely blue head on the art folder stayed true to himself and remained 'different' from his class mates who now work in construction, real estate, and other ordinary jobs. His first design foreshadowed his life. I can only hope that those students who drew the marijuana leaves did not foretell their futures as accurately. I pray for them, trusting they choose to keep their brain cells and have discovered some of their limitless possibilities in life. I also hope they have learned to use their intelligence when they have to make choices, unconsciously remembering their teacher who knew they were smart and capable and did not need to fail the tests that life set for them.

•••

CHAPTER XIX

•••

My personal life has gone through a lot of change and drama since I first started my teaching career.

Two years after my second husband died I married another man whom I loved with an unexpectedly powerful passion. I moved from the low income basement suite into an upper middle class area called High Capilano. The lovely colonial home we owned was like something in a fairy tale. It had French windows and was surrounded by twenty-three huge pine trees. It looked beautiful nestled against the slope of the snow-capped Grouse Mountain.

Bursting from happiness, I felt I had arrived at the top of my life. I had reached my goal to become a classroom teacher. I was living in the country of my dreams. I had two healthy children, and a husband whom I loved more than I could ever have even fantasized about. But life is not a fairy tale. It does not finish with the line: "Lived happily ever after."

My son went to a nearby high school and my little girl to kindergarten. Often Fathers have difficulty coping with their teenage sons. Most Stepfathers are incapable of this. My son was one teenager in a thousand - namely quiet, respectful, hard working and polite. I never had to nag him about homework. Quite the contrary - I had to persuade him to quit studying at two in the morning and to get some rest. All I heard from his teachers was praise. I regularly had to visit his school to see him receive awards.

My husband must have felt jealous of the love and attention I gave my son. He pressed me to send the boy to boarding school. He had never had children of his own, and consequently he could not relate to my feelings. My son seemed to understand the situation and went away for a year. I hoped my marriage would improve with the absence of a teenager at home, but I did not take into consideration the bitterness which would fill my heart.

My daughter, being a little girl, charmed my new husband enough that she did not present an immediate problem. After a year, my son hoped to move back home, but my husband resisted the idea. I wanted to leave and get a separation, but my noble son talked me out of it: "Mom, if you leave him because of me, I am going to feel obligated toward you for a lifetime. You are in love Mom. It is your life. I am going to be just fine even if I live somewhere else," and he did. He moved into the house of a friend whose Mother was a single parent. I paid for his room and board with dollars and for my lessons in life with pain. I have a saying that all of my friends and students know: "I love everybody's children. You can imagine how much I love my own."

Pain and bitterness overshadowed my relationship with my husband and undermined my happiness. I felt resentment toward him. Yet at the same time I loved him with the passion of a woman in full bloom. The more I loved him, the more dissatisfied I became with my own character. I felt ashamed of my love and acted hysterical when we argued.

I wished to have a child with him. I thought it would heal our problems, but this was not written in my book of the future. After two miscarriages, my husband decided he wanted a separation. Fortunately there was still some pride in my tormented soul and I let him go gracefully.

This man had been raised in a male dominated society, and he thought of himself as the one with the right to make decisions without ever having to consult his wife. He was offended by my hysterical rebelliousness and he wisely knew that our marriage was not working. I am grateful to him now. He had the strength to break our love bonds because I was not able to do it.

We sold the dream house and with my share I bought a small home on the outskirts of Vancouver, in a working class area where I felt much more comfortable there then in the area designated for the rich. I moved in to my new place with my daughter, my university student son and our dog. I thought the world had come to an end and that I was never going to smile or laugh again. The incredible pain I felt was not comparable to any suffering I had known before. I would often think how gladly I would exchange the suffering in my heart for physical pain - how much easier that would be to bare.

Even then life had not quit giving me lessons. To my astonishment, I learned I was pregnant again. I felt a sparkle of hope and happiness. Even if I had lost my husband, I would after all have his child to love and live for.

When the familiar cramps came after my third month, I realized there was no hope. One early morning my son drove me to the hospital emergency ward. It was 4 A.M. and my doctor did not arrive until 11 A.M. Until then I lay in a pool of blood and pain that was nothing compared to the suffering in my heart. Around ten, I suddenly felt very light. The pain had all gone, my feelings grew white wings, and my mind was filled with a sudden tolerance and acceptance of what had happened. I decided to get up and look at the blue sky through the window only to realize I could not move. I could not even lift my head or my hands. Then I understood: I was dying.

"Good," I thought. "I do not have to suffer anymore. It is so easy - much easier than I thought. I am going to get on my wings and fly away." Then I remembered my daughter - the little girl just approaching those hard years of puberty. Could I leave her alone? Would that be fair? My love for her saved my life. I gathered whatever tiny strength there was left inside me and pulled the cord placed by my shoulder. The nurse came running. A few hours and several blood transfusions later, I ended up in an operating room.

Three days later, my son and my daughter came to take me home. It was early summer. They were suntanned, young and beautiful. Both of them were wearing white jeans and white shirts. Their smiles and kisses reminded me I had a good life - one filled with hope, love, and beauty.

It took me an incredibly long time to get over my broken marriage emotionally. It was a long and dark road to walk. Every step was painful and every night seemed an eternity locked in loneliness.

My son eventually got married and moved away. My daughter grew to be a teenager and not an easy one. I was still walking on the road of pain. I was smoking two packs of cigarettes a day and drank more than was healthy, but eventually I pulled through. My love for my profession filled my working days and my love for my daughter filled my home life.

I learned slowly and the hard way that it does not matter how low you fall. There is always a way to save your life. Just pick yourself up and walk. Do not hide. Face the pain and face your own weaknesses. Do not blame yourself or others for what has happened. Nothing can change the past, but the future is in your hands. Accept yourself, forgive yourself. Think about your mistakes as lessons to be learned from. Do not feel sorry for yourself; self-pity is humiliating. You must learn to love yourself so you can quit killing your body with cigarettes and alcohol. Don't worry how long it takes. Just proceed one step at a time. In the midst of the darkness, there is a light that can change you, and instead of falling further, it can guide you upward.

My turning point occurred about two years after my separation from my husband. Teaching every day helped kill time and still my burning thoughts. I worked diligently, not noticing how much despair and unhappiness I must have been radiating. Scott, one of my outspoken grade nine students, put up his hand - interrupting my lecture.

"Can't you wait until I've finished?" I shouted. After every class presentation I would ask if there were any questions. The tall boy just looked me straight in the eye and, the rest of the class deadly silent, he asked: "Ms. H., what has happened to you?"

I got irritated: "What do you mean, what has happened to me?"

"You used to be such a loving, kind person and now you are such a bitch!"

I froze, the class did, too. Everybody was looking at us. I stood there for a long moment until my eyes started to fill with tears. "You are right, my son," I answered when I found my voice. "I am acting like a bitch because I am bitter. My husband left me and it's hard on me, you know," I told the class honestly. They accepted that and they forgave me.

That was the light that turned me around. It took me years to emerge from the despair, but after that day I changed toward my students. I listened to their problems so I could forget my own. I talked about how valuable and unique they were, helping them to raise their self-esteem when I really needed to raise mine. I would point out the beauty of life - of nature, art, animals, plants, and people - just to keep those values clear for myself. I loved and cared about my students so I would receive their love and care in return.

Finally I arrived at the sunny hill top where I am sitting now. Since then I have often wondered how much these students learned from me. I hope they gained something because I have learned a lot from my pupils, every day I have been a teacher. I hope I will be able to teach and learn until the day when I no longer have any reason to keep on living and I am ready to grow those white wings which will finally carry me away.

•••

CHAPTER XX

•••

Society has never changed as much and as fast as it has in my generation's life-time.

When my grandmother was young, teenagers did not have the right to question their parents' values. They were expected to obey without thinking. If they had any doubts, they hid them and felt guilty. Strong moral codes, which society and religions conditioned them to believe, did not leave much room for individual-ity. Marriage was unshakable - a strong fortress of morals - and couples married for life. Not having any sex education, most of the middle and upper class girls walked to the altar completely unaware of the physical aspects of their commit-ment. The more 'innocent' they were, the more proud their parents were of them. Parents strongly believed that girls did not need much education beyond learn-ing to read and write. They were trained to sew, embroider, play a little piano and look upon a man as a hero - a stronghold of future security. Men had the privilege of possessing brains. Ladies were supposed to be innocent, cute, pretty, and dumb.

The daughters of the peasants were better off. They had opportunities to learn the facts of life from observing their environment. Most of them married for love, unlike the 'lucky' rich girls who were rarely allowed to follow their hearts. Their future husbands were selected by the family. In the selection process, prosperity and financial security were considered first, not the emotions of the young couple. It was thought that physical attraction would lead to trouble and that the best marriages were based on duty. Parents said of their children: "They will get used to each other and love will develop later."

The lack of birth control and sex education motivated parents to try to marry off their daughters as soon as they physically ripened. They cared nothing about emotional maturity. No wonder so many brides ran home in horror and bewil-derment after their wedding nights. They thought their husbands had turned into monsters demanding what seemed a shameful, disgusting act. The elderly ladies of the family would smile knowingly and shake their heads happily gossip-ing with each other. "Oh the little innocent dove, she will acquire a taste for the 'shameful act' eventually."

Those poor young brides of my grandma's generation - they were just teenagers. By the time they reached their late twenties, they would have three or four children and were bound to husbands they often hated. In the best of situations, the brides did get used to their marriage partners, but in either case they were trapped.

Brides acquired a taste for life, all right. Their mature, womanly feelings were usually wrapped around a fantasy - a man of their dreams, a true love whom they could never touch or, God save us, make love to. Ladies went to bed dutifully with their husbands and dreamed about somebody else. What a hypocritical world!

By the time my mother's generation grew up, divorce had become an alternative, even if it was not acceptable by the moral standards of society. If the man disposed of his wife, usually in favour of a new and more exciting woman, the reason given for the separation would be: "My wife did not want to perform her marriage duty." This meant she did not want to make love as often as he, or did not like the ways he wanted her to perform. Society would nod in sympathy for the poor husband who worked the whole day to provide for his family, but had no pity for the cruel and cold wife who had neglected her 'marriage duty'. In this male dominated society, divorced wives became social outcasts. Without professional training, they ended up working at low paid jobs, struggled with poverty, and raised their children alone.

Naturally women tried their best to stay married to preserve their status and financial security, for the sake of their children. They enslaved themselves, giving up their personalities, their will, and their happiness for the 'gods' they called husbands. It was common in my Mom's day for a woman to address her spouse as 'my Lord' or 'my Commander'.

I grew up with that concept myself, but I questioned it, as I questioned almost all the moral values of my childhood society. Maybe that's why I ended up a twice-divorced woman, unlike all my nieces and cousins in the old country who have lived all their lives with their first husbands. I can trace my family tree back to the seventeenth century. Nobody before me had ever gotten divorced. There were widows - yes - but not one broken marriage. This makes me the 'black sheep' of my family, the one who left the old ways and ventured out to a dangerous new world.

I respect and love my relatives in the old country and they in turn love but also envy me. In their eyes I am brave for having broken free from the old traditions and common fears. Their way of life is now different from mine. I can't see myself ever holding on to a marriage that offers daily suffering and frustration. Two of my cousins live like that. They are very unhappy, but they keep their families together. In addition to the financial considerations, these women have strong feelings of duty towards their children. I can relate to that and salute to their heroism.

Divorce is hard on the partners involved, but it is even harder on the children. In the eyes of a small child, Mother and Father are Gods. Divorce brutally shatters a child's heaven. Nobody is a winner in such a drama. Yet, is the solution to stay together? Fighting parents create a hell for their children, too. Battered family lives leave life-long scars. Sometimes it is better to grow up with one parent than with two who pull the children in different directions. The problem is as complex as life itself.

In schools, teachers deal with teenagers who are suffering immensely because of family break up. It is hard for children to accept that their Mothers and Fathers are common people - not gods, but humans with faults and weaknesses, victims of their failed expectations.

The world is changing for the better, but every step forward has its own hazards. No longer expected to endure the traditional unbreakable marriages, people now can choose their mates freely. They even have the opportunity to live together on a trial basis. How is it, then, that there are so many bad marriages and so many divorces?

I have a theory which is only my personal view and not to be mistaken for an unshakable truth. In our society, young people are victims of the media's unrealistic image of love. Harlequin romances, soap operas, Hollywood love movies, magazine pictures and articles - all these portray loving couples who waited to get married and then lived happily ever after. In real life this very rarely happens.

Schools provide teaching in math and physics and have children spend innumerable hours learning theories and giving tests. But we forget to teach children about the true nature of humans and to guide them towards self-discovery and self-acceptance. Sex education is still handled with kid gloves, beating around the bush rather than making young people face life as it really is.

Love is the magical word under which they collect a great variety of things to confuse the youth. Because of the pictures in Playboy Magazine, which present only bodies made to look perfect with make up and photographic trickery, young men are disappointed by their first real life experiences. Young ladies should also watch out. Married life is not like those bridal magazine pictures, and the honeymoon is over too soon. If a couple enters their shared life with unrealistic expectations, disillusionment will be just around the corner. Bitterness, resentment, arguments and hostility will soon take the place of the earlier love.

When parents become unhappy, their children get caught between them. They love Mom and they love Dad, but the parents do not love each other. The situation is even worse when one partner has stopped loving and the other still hopelessly pursues it. Young people are shaken to the core by seeing their Mother cry or drink to drown her despair and their Father stays away from the house until the day when he officially moves out. Whose side can the children take? Who is right? Who is wrong? Even if they blame one parent, their hearts will bleed because of the hate.

The secure home they knew is not the same anymore. One very important person is missing. It is even worse if the family has to move. Children, like old people, are very attached to their childhood scenery. Settling down in a new environment makes them miserable and depressed for a long time.

As bad as the situation has become for them, the worst is still ahead. This happens when Mom starts to date another man or Dad introduces a new lady to them. If the children are very small, it is easier. The older the children, the more difficult it is to get them to accept the fact that Mother or Father is sharing their bed with a stranger.

The new boyfriend or girlfriend can be a wonderful person, but a teenager will still look upon them with the most critical eyes. Actions that the real father or mother could get away with, make adolescents bitter for they have no tolerance, no forgiveness, no love to give the intruder. "The creep, I hate him/her." Inside their hearts teens harbour a rosy image of a lost parent and believe he or she would act differently.

Ironically, Step-parents can have similar feelings of resentment toward their new family. "How happy we would be, if only we didn't have to put up with that impossible teenager!"

The result of all this is that the biological parents will be caught between their love for their children and their love for their new mates. When forced to take sides, they will always end up generating resentment and anger in their partner or their children. Being ground between these jealous opposing forces will make life a nightmare. I know that sometimes, in very few cases, step-parenting works out, but unfortunately this takes much more acceptance, tolerance, and love than many of us possess.

After my divorce I found myself in this situation. Having a teenage daughter and trying to find a new partner who would love me and love my child the same way I do, meant that I set myself up for new hurts. I was raised with the common belief that a woman's place is beside a man. My evenings became aimless, and my nights were empty.

We should teach our children from the beginning of their lives to value solitude. Like the native Indians do, we could send our youngsters to spend a day or two alone with nature. We ought to teach them to spend their time meaningfully without having to look for approval from others. The image of the couple holding hands and walking into the sunset on a beach under the palm trees is misleading. If you ask a teenager to draw or paint a landscape, one out of ten is going to draw the above described or some similar romantic scene.

It would be more encouraging for the young's future if the media emphasized the beauty and value of a person walking on the beach alone and listening to their own thoughts. Perhaps we should teach meditation techniques to small children.

To share moments with somebody we love is very special, but it is equally special to have exceptional moments by ourselves. Why does the advertising industry not present solitude in as glamorous and desirable a manner as partnership? I think it must be because the notion still exists from our past that a woman can be happy only if she has a husband or at least a boyfriend. In my mother's time unmarried women had no respect. "Something must be wrong with her. She is alone," people would say. This conditioning by society has created much unhappiness and many tragedies.

Even nowadays many woman who are over thirty and who never married wish that they would have. Would they feel better if you told them the story of your own marriage - the frustrations, the arguments, and the abuse you endured while you were tied to a person who was not the right match for you? Single women will say to you, "Oh, yes, I know. That's why I chose to be alone." But in their hearts they will envy you even for your struggles. At least you got to walk down the aisle, and you had the right to call yourself Mrs. instead of Miss. Why do they feel like that? Because of the expectations of the society created by centuries of conditioning.

Why don't we teach our children the facts from birth? We are all different. What is good for one person need not apply to another. Some people are better off if they never marry. It is all right to be yourself and follow your individual desires.

It took me long years to learn the value of solitude and to shake off the false expectations of life that my family had taught me to believe in. At present I am living alone by choice, but I still feel funny about walking into a restaurant or a theatre without a man as an escort. Am I ever going to shake off my conditioning?

The world is changing for the better. Society tends to be more open-minded and tolerant of individual choice. It is O.K. to live together. It is O.K. to be single and have a child. Yet parents still press their children to grow up and live up to the expectations set by the family.

We could speed up the change in schools by teaching self-discovery. In addition to those over-emphasized academic subjects, schools should offer a course like 'The Exploration of the Self,' or a subject like 'Communication', meaning learning to interact with others. At the University of California, Leo Buscaglia teaches 'Love'. Sex is after all a form of communication - an extension of our feelings toward another person. It is a language like music, dance, or painting. We should openly teach the young generation the difference between love and the physical satisfaction of sexual excitement that has no connection to caring, tender feelings. Let young people realize there is a need in everybody for physical excitement, and then help them learn to judge for themselves the difference between love and sexual pleasure. How many movies hypocritically say their subject is love when all they depict is sexual hunger.

Lots of hurts could be avoided by talking openly about our body needs and helping the young sort out their feelings without guilt. Physical attraction has tricked so many people into marriage and later left them empty, disillusioned and blaming one another. If learning to distinguish between genuine love and infatuation, between reality and illusions, was an essential skill for choosing a life time mate, there would be fewer marriages, of course, and much less divorce. Understanding the meaning of unconditional love would avoid many errors in pair selection: "Do I love that person as she or he really is? Would I love him/her even if the physical body were damaged? In sickness and in poverty? Can I possibly spend the rest of my life every day with that same person?"

In our marriage vows we say those heavy words: "Until death do us part." But very few of us consider them deeply enough. There is usually no time. Brides and grooms are too busy planning the details of the ceremony, the dresses for the bridesmaids, the choice of flowers, the invitation list and practising the walk down the aisle. Everybody around them focuses on the honeymoon rather than on the life ahead. Who tries to picture themselves losing a job, paying bills, working from morning to night and then just falling into bed to sleep? Which of you imagined at your own marriage a day when your teenage daughter went out with an idiot, or your beloved son, the pride of the family, failed in school, tried shoplifting, or started taking drugs? Will you and your partner have enough love to support each other and not blame the other if your child fails? Does your heart beat faster when your partner reaches out to touch even though you have shared your bed for many years? It is possible, but relationships require hard work and people must make the right choices at the beginning.

The most important foundations for a good marriage are: first, self-knowledge and self-acceptance, and then knowing and accepting the other person. Self-discovery is a life time task. You are learning and growing all through your life, unless you get stuck somewhere along the road or, instead of concentrating on steering your vehicle forward, you keep your eyes on the past.

People have unlimited potential as do their partners. Only if they know themselves and love themselves as they are, do they have the chance to accept and cherish another for the person he or she is.

What keeps people together when they obviously lack the above qualities? The fear of being alone, mutual financial investments, social image, the duty to raise the children - those are strong reasons. They carry great weight in life, but they should not be good enough to force someone to settle for a limited life or the humiliation of giving up their true personality. Unless you find a mate who will accept you one hundred percent the way you really are, he/she is not worth life-long commitment. What is wrong with a short term romance? We should advise our children to take the time to be selective and not to marry out of desperation.

If the new generation grows up with self-knowledge and the freedom to decide their own preferences, there will be fewer marriages and fewer children. The world is over-populated anyway, and it would be better to avoid the births of millions of children who would otherwise grow up in miserable families.

Since my grandparents' lifetimes society's standards for love and marriage have changed for the better. Of that I am convinced. There is much more tolerance toward single parents. A woman now does not have to commit suicide because of an accidental pregnancy. But there is still lots left to do. Let's hope that the next fifty years bring with them as much change as the previous fifty. With the right guidance teenagers of the future can become the masters of their own lives, make conscientious choices, and abandon fear. Let's work for a future where love motivates the actions of people instead of fear.

•••

CHAPTER XXI

•••

"A Little Girl"

There was once a girl
who sat down
and decided to write
a story about her life.
She called it 'Failure'.
Dark and alone,
where there is no cure.
Deep inside where
secrets hide.
No hearts of love
can see her through.
crying, clawing.
Hoping someone will
come and keep
her warm and secure.
But! The world is cruel.
Leaving no routes
except that for one.
How tempting it is,
to just back away
and shrink down to size!
So, this little girl
decided to play.
Taking a scarf.
She hung it from
the bedroom light.
Each day she watched it,
Swinging back and forth,
wandering when someone

would shake her awake.
Squeezing her harder.
She could not wait,
so instead like a bubble
she burst . . .
And met her fate.
Taking the scarf,
Forming a noose,
she put her head through.
And then hung
like a doll,
Forever limp and lifeless.
The End.

By: Neelam Mann   Grade: 10

This poem was written by Neelam, a grade ten art student, fifteen years old - only a decade from her girlhood world of *Mary had a Little Lamb.* For this girl the magical, sweet nursery had transformed into an empty space with walls that caged the human soul with loneliness.

What happened to her spirit?

Our world is warm and secure as long as we see our parents as gods keeping us safe, no matter what.

In North American society, most newborns have their own room adorably decorated for them by adults. Pictures of Disney characters and fairy tale figures, boxes and shelves loaded with toys, and pink, blue, or white backgrounds for the bright colours of the plastic toys - parents are keen to provide a happy environment for their babies. Everybody is smiling; everybody is kind. The child gets the impression he is the most important person in the world and everything revolves around him. After all children receive loads of toys on every possible occasion. Isn't that wonderful? Loving parents, not sweet baby toys are what children really need.

The more sophisticated a toy is, the less room it leaves for imagination. I remember all the fancy dressed dolls with flowers adorning their bonnets that were given to me by my Mom. I hated them. I could not play with them. They sat lifelessly on a shelf. I tolerated them because I did not want to hurt my Mother's feelings.

In the happy times of the summer holidays which I spent at my Grandma's country estate, the old lady who was the cook there made me dolls from corncobs. She dressed them with scraps of fabric and painted on simple black dot eyes with big eyelashes for the girl doll and a long mustache for the boy. She used a burned stick from the stove to create her art work. The corner of an empty chicken coop became the doll's house. Empty boxes made splendid beds and chairs. I picked flowers and put them into a chipped glass for the table. On those long summer days, my doll house gave me a world of my own.

I loved my corncob dolls dearly and my heart shattered into a million painful pieces when my Mom fed the fireplace with my precious friends at the end of the summer. She looked at me in surprise: "What are you crying for? You have Amalia and Theodora to play with." I'd maliciously given names that I did not like to the fancy dolls.

I tried to defend my executed friends. "But Pici and Paci," as I lovingly called them, "were real." Did Mom not see how expressive their eyes were? "Pici and Paci?" she said. "What ridiculous names those are for corncobs. Anyway they have dried out and would leave dirt all over the Persian carpets at home." That was the end of it. Those carpets were obviously more important than my raggedy corn dolls, too dirty from playing in the old chicken coop. They would have been outcasts in the world of velvet upholstery and oriental carpets. After that I took to drawing my own dolls on paper and painting on them the big black eyes with long lashes of Pici and long moustache of Paci. I'd cut them out and hide them in a shoe box under my bed.

One uncle, who was the black sheep of our family having caused my respectable grandparents lots of shame, secretly was my best friend. My child's mind could not understand why everybody kept rolling their eyes and throwing up their hands whenever my uncle's doings were the topic of conversation. They spoke about him in their German "Nicht for dem kind" talk. I loved him dearly.

He was fun to be with. He never told me to be careful with my white stockings or not kneel in the dirt. One day after a summer heavy rainstorm we took off our shoes and went for a walk. For a happy hour we splashed in the mud. He lifted me up onto his shoulder so I could 'steal' the fruit from an apple tree. He just wiped the partially ripened apples off with his sleeves and we ate them. Those apples' excellent sour, crunchy taste has stayed with me throughout my life. Even now I do not buy sweet apples - just green ones.

I confided my childhood secrets in this uncle and even showed him my paper Pici and Paci. He told me that they were absolutely beautiful and said I could be sure they were the same as the corncob dolls because when my Mother had burned them, their spirits had remained with me. Their spirits could not leave me because of our love for each other and now happily occupied the bodies I had made.

My uncle made me furniture from match boxes. I drew pillows and quilts and cut them out for the bed. The dresser had real drawers that pulled out with wool knob handles so I could put paper clothes inside. I could set up my doll house under the table sheltered by the long tablecloth 'walls'.

Fifty years ago the toy industry was not as sophisticated as it is now. Still life-like or realistic toys managed even then to weigh down the wings of my imagination. With the toy industry now manufacturing so many technical wonders what room is left for fantasy and creativity?

Computers, video games, walking and talking dolls, cars and motorcycles - all the things adults 'play with' are provided in miniature versions for children. Advertising on television creates a craving for these products in children, just as it does in adults for material possessions. Dad thinks about the run down, fifteen year old family car and wishes for a new four wheel drive. Mom would like to go on a cruise glamorously dressed like the people on the T.V. screen. Their teenage boy dreams about the electrifying feel of a Camero and all the girls who would love to ride with him if he had one. The little one nags Mom to buy him the latest science fiction character, whose weapon will defend humans against the alien invasion.

We can't shut T.V. and the effects of advertisements out of our lives. It is not possible to ignore sophisticated toys and give everybody corncobs to play with. We are all different and what makes one child happy is not necessarily joyful to another. All I would like to say is that parents should be careful of what they buy. They should take the time to get to know the person they gave life to and try to avoid projecting their tastes and desires onto their children.

Adults should experiment with the toys they buy or give their children the opportunity to choose according to their own interests. Allow a child's interest to build before he gets a new present and then watch to see if he is really happy with it. Does he play with the new possession for days, or months, or is it only a short time before the novelty has worn off?

Most children have the desire to create a world of their own. Parents should buy helpful tools and toys that will encourage their creativity and then not worry if the child's room looks messy and is not colour co-ordinated.

Well before he had learned how to read, all my son wanted were books and magazines. I had to buy comics and he'd look at the pictures over and over until the story would reveal itself to him. Reading to him gave us some of our best times together. He never got tired of listening, and when he himself learned to read, it was hard to drag him away from his desk. Consequently, his room was full of books and his desk was covered with 'very important' papers.

Instead of reading, my daughter preferred inventing stories and telling them while vigorously acting out the roles of her characters. She created dramatic confrontations between a sweet little bunny rabbit and a monster. Fortunately her stories usually ended with the monster's realization of his own self-worth and his holding hands with the bunny as they danced off into the sunset. Consequently, my daughter's room was a messy place that provided all her imaginary friends space to hide, to play, to fight, and to dance.

It is not easy to be a parent. Many people go to driving school before they sit behind the steering wheel of a car and learn a trade before they occupy a job, but who is trained to be a parent? Where is the school in which young couples can learn how to raise another human being before they become parents?

My training for motherhood is rooted in my own childhood memories. Every time I experienced humiliation or injustice as a child, I made a mental note: "I am not going to do that with my child." I am sure other children do the same, but unfortunately, most of us forget. Early bitter memories are buried under the events of the passing years. The conditioning influences of our environment - parents, school, and church - mould us into a likeness of the previous generation. When it is our turn, instead of taking different approaches, we just follow the old patterns.

At an early age working with other children who talked about personal problems helped to keep my memories fresh and I have turned my promises into reality. This worked wonders for me in my own teaching and parenting. My children think of me as a trusted friend, who understands them completely and loves them unconditionally. Although I could never afford to stay home and devote my time just to child raising, our limited time together became special.

The ten year age difference between my children kept me a long time at the task of being a 'good Mother'. Their different characters challenged me to handle them as individuals. My son, being a studious, task-oriented, hard working teenager who never lied to get out of the consequences of his actions, often left me feeling Bohemian and not serious enough by comparison. My daughter on the other hand chose the ways of a bright and rebellious spirit and tried all the routes teenagers walk to challenge the world around them.

I made plenty of mistakes while I tried to guide my children toward adulthood. I do not claim to know all the answers for the problems of parenting, but I still feel qualified to reflect on the ways that worked for me in hopes of helping others raise their own children.

Here are a few tips:

- Think of your newborn as an independent person with a given character and not like a wax figure you can mould with your own expectations. You can influence your child, but not change him to your liking by force.
- Watch for the first signs of your baby's personality. The new soul will very early give away clues to his or her basic nature.
- Respect your child as another human being who has the full right to be himself as you have the right to be yourself.
- Do not ever ridicule your child's actions. He is locked inside a small body, and he has to learn how to walk, talk, and communicate with the surrounding world.
- Listen to your child seriously and attentively when she or he talks. Do not assume baby talk is just play that does not make sense. Showing an interest in everything your child 'tells' you

will create a basis for trust and honesty in the later years when your child becomes a teenager. Try to understand.

- Never wish your children would do things you are not modelling for him/her yourself. It is unlikely that your son will turn into a scholar if you never open a book yourself. It is unfair of you to preach not to drink, smoke, or behave violently if you are not living by your own rules. Sometimes young people learn those habits by hating the weaknesses of their parents. But what a way to learn! The parents' negative behaviour is an excuse for a child to slide into drug related dependency.

- Let your child make his own choices even when they contradict your best advice. Make him understand that you will be there to help even if his choice turns out to be a disaster. Always back up your child because your love for him is worth more to him than anything else.

- Last, but not least, express your love for your children often, not just when they are sweet little kids, but also when they reach adolescence. This is the time when they most need assurance.

The transition from the fairy tale-like nursery of a child to the prison-like teenage room where Neelam's character hanged herself is a story of the love lost. Your child will grow from a sweet little baby into a fourteen year old whose face is covered with acne and who is awkward and withdrawn. The time from the infant's magical sweetness to the misery of adolescence is so short - too short for Mom and Dad to adjust to the changes. It is hard to believe that your daughter is already interested in boys and your son is thinking about sex. They are ashamed of their feelings, their fantasies, and their desires. They do not talk about these feelings in front of their parents. Mom and Dad would not understand. In this way children start to question authority, challenge the rules of the family, and end up hiding behind music turned up full blast to avoid conversations.

Mother and Father feel hurt by the seemingly disrespectful behaviour. They feel cheated by life. "I gave up so much for my children and spent all my time and money to raise them. Instead of travelling or buying nice things, we sacrificed everything. Now they only listen to their good-for-nothing friends. They question our authority, and experiment with sex and drugs." The list of complaints and hurts is long on both sides. The generation gap widens until the teenager find himself alone.

Most of the troublemakers, the so called cool ones, are heartbreakingly lonely kids who have lost the security of their parent's love. They still seek that love though for the more they act out, the more obvious it is that they're crying out for help: "Love me, accept me, listen to me, please!"

They misbehave just to be the centre of attention even when the consequence is punishment. If a teacher sends them to the office or they're suspended, their parents have to come in to talk to the principal, and that's good. Anything is better than not being heard, not being noticed, being ignored, or being entrapped by loneliness.

Parents who do not notice these danger signs, or do not act to break down the barriers by showing understanding, tolerance and love, will be lucky if their teenagers remain only rowdy. Some go much further and attempt suicide. Very few of them really mean to die. They just want to do something so terrible that all attention will turn towards them. If a suicide attempt succeeds, the lonely soul's loveless cry burns marks that never heal into the parent's spirit. Why wait for that to happen? Why not put aside your pride and come down from the pedestal of parental authority and become the loving friend of your teenager?

Do not be shocked if your daughter loses her virginity when she is only thirteen. Do not spank your child because he smoked marijuana. Do not ever say: "This is my house. You will live by my rules or . . ." Instead make it clear your home is your child's home, a place where he can always find love and understanding. It is perfectly natural for children to have an interest in forbidden things. Point out the dangers and step back. Let your teenagers decide whether to try or not to try. It is better for them to have a few bad experiences than be forever alienated. Young people are bright and learn fast. If they experiment and the results are what you said was going to happen, they will realize that Mom and Dad were right after all. If they know you will take them back into your arms, they will run to the safety of your love, rather than blame you for their bad experiences.

I started this chapter with one of my students' poems, and I am going to finish it with another. Tim was fifteen years old when he wrote this:

Youth is a Time When

Youth is a time when you are very small.
And people just do not care,
Young is like not being there,
Being left out.

Youth is a time when people don't want you until you're
                    older.
The time when you're not a kid.

Youth is a time when you must go to school.
And put up with the other kids picking on you.
Not being able to do what you want in your life.

Youth is a time when you get into fights.
To go through the pain of someone hitting you.
Or you hitting someone else.

Youth is a time when there is no escape.
No escape, then to just enjoy being a kid.

Tim Schneider

•••

CHAPTER XXII

•••

One afternoon, the last student had left the art room and I sat behind my desk to rest for a few minutes. Sitting down for a length of time is not part of an art teacher's schedule - that is not if she takes her job seriously. I walk from student to student throughout the day, helping or just talking. By the time I leave the school, it is getting dark outside, and I still have to pick up groceries before I drive home.

Usually my daughter would arrive at the house well before I did. That day as I stepped out of the car in the front of the house, I could hear the sound of the blasting stereo. My living room was packed with teenagers drinking Coke and smoking cigarettes. I had to step over their outstretched legs clothed in ragged jeans and torn sneakers. Students of the late seventies made worn clothing fashionable. New and immaculate clothes were just not 'cool'. Only 'nerds' wore them.

Most of the kids in the house did not even notice my arrival. I considered myself lucky because I had been 'accepted'. "Ms. H. is O.K. She fits right in," as one of them stated. My daughter ran to me for a hug and gave me soft little kisses. Some of her friends followed her example seeing we are a huggy-huggy, kissy-kissy family.

My fridge was empty as usual. No amount of iced tea, Coke or peanut butter sandwiches would last when my daughter's friends were there.

I had already packed away the hand embroidered table cloths. Cigarette burns and Coke glass rings in the furniture had taught me not the care about the appearance of my living room. My furniture looked as worn as my young friends clothes. The multicoloured design of the wall-to-wall carpet mercifully hid the traces of the kids' potato chips and other 'health food' favourites. It was just as if my grade nine class had followed me home. I lived and breathed with teenagers all through my daughter's high school years. Her gang hung out at my place day after day.

"Why on earth do you put up with that?" most of my friends asked, horrified when they saw how I spent my afternoons and evenings.

"Well," I would explain, "they are my daughter's friends and if I didn't let them stay here, they would probably hang out somewhere else where I can't see what's going on. At least I know where my daughter is."

In grade eight, kids still have some of the innocence of childhood left and listen to their Mom's, but by grade nine, suddenly their friends' opinions matter more than anything else. Teens want to belong - to be accepted by their peers, and their Mom's words fall on deaf ears.

Against the advice of my friends, I continued all those years to allow my home to be used as a base for a group of teenagers. And what a group they were! If I had collected around me in my own high school years a group of needy teenagers, my daughter did the same and more. Kids from broken families or from group homes and boys with police records or nowhere else to sleep found their way into my daughter's heart. Some of my pots and blankets were donated to help out. One lad, Ken, lived on his own in a run down apartment house where the communal washroom was at the end of the hallway and the ceilings were peeling because the rain dripped through. My daughter took me to help Ken move into this horrible place. He shared it with other youths who all seemed to feel themselves outside the bounds of our well organized society. I was not surprised when Ken's torn jeans and worn spider web thin T-shirt showed up in my washer and dryer. "But Mom, where can he wash his clothing? There is no warm water where he lives." Ken was watching T.V. in my living room, wrapped in my daughter's housecoat, waiting for the only outfit he had to dry. Naturally we shared our dinner with him.

I would plan to cook for two, but most often ended up feeding a group of hungry kids. They were my daughter's friends and my choices were to either put up with them or show them the door. Knowing my daughter's strong will and character, I decided not to risk her walking out the door after her friends.

So I learned to sleep with the stereo blasting Frank Zappa's 'mild and modest' songs. I valued my daughter's friendship and trust in me more than a quiet, immaculate home. It was not easy, but it was not as hard as you might think. I sat down with the young people, listened to their problems, and laughed at their jokes. They trusted me and asked my opinions about lots of things.

Only her new friends looked horrified when my daughter introduced me by saying: "This is my Mom. She's a teacher, but she is the best!" Soon they were saying they would like to be in my class, in the same way my students in the school often expressed their desire to be my daughter or my son.

So I 'sacrificed' my evenings and my personal life. What man is willing to court a lady who, instead of sitting beside the fireplace and listening to him talk, surrounds herself with a group of teenagers? During those years I often thought about how lucky I was to be single. If my ex-husband had not left me years before, he would certainly have at that time or my daughter would have been one of those runaways. In my experience most students who live in group homes ended up there because Mom's husband or Dad's new wife couldn't stand being with a rotten, disrespectful teenager.

I put up with everything in the name of love, and I got my rewards. Number 1 - My daughter outgrew the world of loud music and the need to hang around with a gang and has become a well educated lady. In spite of her previous 'I hate school' attitude, she attends university, holds a part time job, has travelled extensively in Europe using her own savings, and has kept on understanding and loving people. Number 2 - I learned more from those years of providing a home for teenagers than I ever learned from the child psychology classes at the university. Number 3 - I have true friends. The phone calls, Christmas cards, and visits I receive from young people prove my choice was right. "You should not spend so much money on me," I protested when one of my ex-prot'eg'es brought me three dozen long stemmed roses for my birthday. "Because you care," he put his feelings simply and gave me a shy bear hug.

Choices! These are the keys to future happiness and fulfilment in life. I believe we should start to teach our kids to make their own choices from the cradle.

Our love toward children is so deceptive. We all tend to make choices for them to save them from problems. After all, we are adults, so we know better. However by making choices for children, we are limiting their ability to take responsibility. Obviously when you have a newborn, you have to take charge of every aspect of the baby's life. Even then a Mother could feed on demand and not enforce a sleep schedule, but go with the individual need of her baby contrary to what is often written in books. As our children grow older, we often fail to loosen our control and begin to desire obedience. When the child becomes a teenager, suddenly we expect the young one to be responsible and take charge of his/her life almost overnight. We are getting upset when he or she acts irresponsibly.

From a sheltered childhood, the young one enters junior high school, which is a large jungle that very few thirteen year olds are ready to face. Instead of one mother-like classroom teacher, they see seven or eight different subject teachers, all of whom have tremendous knowledge to offer. But since each teacher sees 175 to 210 students a day, personal contact is almost impossible.

The grade nine and ten students call the new entrants 'babies' and at best look down at them or at worst put them through 'initiations'. The new students feel humiliated and inferior. They face being pushed, shoved, teased, and even being beaten up unless they become leaders or tough kids.

Teachers while presenting theories and facts expect these youngsters to pay attention and work diligently though they often fail to see any connection between school work and their everyday lives. At home Mother and Father preach about responsibility and then just release their children into the confusing world called high school. Without taking into consideration their children's personal interest or lack of interest in a subject, parents want them to bring home good marks and excel.

On the top of all of this confusion, teens' bodies are acting up, too. The girls have to get used to monthly periods, and their growing breasts attract the attention of the boys. The boys wake up with strange feelings. Their fantasies paint feverish pictures about girls and sex. Playboy magazines hidden under the bed by older brothers, love scenes on T.V. programs, and the giggling of the girls next to them in class do not help either. Help . . .!

If we parents made the effort to refrain from making choices for our children and let them suffer the consequences of their bad decisions, they would be better prepared for high school and adolescent life. I do not suggest you should sit back and let a child tumble into a situation that will obviously lead to disaster. I am telling you rather to talk to your child and ask why he wants to do that and what he feels inside? Make him feel safe and trusted so he can say what is on his mind without being afraid of punishment or resentment. Point out patiently why you oppose the choice and what the probable outcome will be if he goes ahead. Say it as loving, friendly advice only. Avoid forcing your opinion on the child. If he chooses to go ahead regardless, he has to take the consequences, too.

It is very hard to step back and let your beloved son or daughter do something that will bring him/her harm. In the long run, your reward will come. Your child won't be able to blame you if he took the wrong step. It was his own doing, and after a few bad choices he will listen to your advice voluntarily.

How many people do you know who blame others for their misfortune? Lots of us think if we had made different decisions, we would now be better off. It might be true or might not, but parents, friends or teachers whose advice led us to unhappiness are seldom forgiven. We forgive ourselves more readily.

It is amusing how many people talk their way into others' lives. They know everything. Where do they get their confidence? Probably from ignorance. These 'know-it-all' friends are the ones to avoid when advice is needed. What is true for one person is not necessarily true for another. It is smarter to ask somebody who tends to say: "I do not know. You have to do what you feel is right." If you insist, this person might give you an example of what they did in a similar situation and tell you honestly the outcome of their actions.

So many of my 'friends' gave me opinions I had not asked for regarding my daughter's upbringing: "She has too much freedom! I would not let her have friends like those. I would not let her smoke, go to a rock concert, stay out late, and so forth." If I had followed their advice and my rebellious, hot-headed child had run away, disappeared, or (God save every Mother from this fate) committed suicide, what would they have said? "Oh, we knew she was going to end up like that. Her mother did not discipline her." Like so many others she would have become just a bad statistic.

Every child is different. Some follow their parents' direction; others rebel. The obedient child is not necessarily the good child. Sometimes the brightest and most talented people were hell raisers in their adolescent years.

Would any child you know run away or commit suicide if parental love and understanding were unconditional? Did your daughter lose her virginity, get pregnant, do drugs, steal money? What can a teenager do that you as a Mother or Father can't forgive? Who is going to help your children if you, the parent, abandon them? Is your pride more important to you than your child?

I made mistakes, too. Sometimes I could not hold myself back and tried to guide forcefully, but in the long run I accepted it when my children decided to choose a different road.

I have only a few rules that I have tried to model myself. They are love, acceptance, and honesty. I told my children many times: "Please do not lie. There is no need to. You can't do anything I don't want to hear about. If there is a problem, out with it. I won't be horrified. I won't faint." I made it clear I was the one they could count on. I lived by that rule and it worked. It made my life easier. No secrets were kept behind my back.

Parents sometimes imagine their daughter is an angel, or close to one, and in the meantime she is contemplating suicide. Fearing her parents more than the consequences of her actions, she cannot tell them what she has done.

"Mom, the principal is going to phone you. I skipped out of school three days in a row," my daughter said one day - very matter of fact. With a calm facial expression I asked, without raising my voice: "Why did you skip? Don't I let you stay home whenever you feel really sick of school?" "Oh, there's no thrill in staying home. That's boring. My girlfriend and I went window shopping downtown and we saw such a beautiful sweater. Do you think you could buy it for me, please?" She looked at me with her large blue eyes and all my inner anger evaporated. I felt like laughing. "Well, I do not think it was right to skip school and certainly when they phone I will tell them you were not sick. You'll have to face the consequences. Serving detention will not kill you. We'll talk about that sweater another time."

This is just one example of how I handled such situations. Some of our 'never lie' talks were much more difficult hurdles to get over because of my great concern for the safety of my child. In the long run however, we managed with flying colours, and my children became my best friends. I have repaid their honesty with the same. We can talk about absolutely anything. There is no subject we cannot discuss.

In school I use the same tactics. I tell the students to be honest and not to lie. "I can take the truth, just try me." And they do.

"You are ten minutes late for class. Where have you been?"

"You know, Ms. H., the vice principal was talking to me. I could not interrupt him."

"O.K. Where is your late note?"

"He did not give me one."

"I see. You know what, son? I will ask him and if you lied I will never believe you again. You will lose all your credibility."

"No, Ms. H. I'm sorry! I was talking to my friend in the washroom."

"That's better. I appreciate your honesty. Now you can help me wash the paintbrushes after school and the next time you want to talk to your friend, ask my permission first. If nothing important is going on, I will excuse you for a few minutes."

It works. I do not think that more students leave my classes than those of the other teachers, and at least I know what they are up to. Lying develops bad character. It is more harmful to the child than my breaking a few rigid school rules.

Tom is a notorious skipper. The vice principal came to ask me about his attendance record. "He is fine - always here." I answered. Later I confronted the boy: "What do I hear Tom? You miss most of your classes? How come you do not skip mine?"

"Why would I?" he answered. "Your class is fun and if I badly want a smoke, you always let me go anyway." I was glad the vice principal left before Tom's statement. I am not sure he would have appreciated my classroom policy regarding honesty.

•••

CHAPTER XXIII

•••

Our school system lags behind the times. Life has changed so much since my high school years, but the traditional ways of education mostly remain.

There is always something new being offered - the curriculum has been re-written several times - but the way we teach the current generation needs a total overhaul instead of minor changes. The computer has brought many new possibilities into our classrooms. A handful of enthusiastic teachers are trying to create a universal curriculum to teach global awareness and world citizenship. Yet in everyday school life not that much has changed. Teachers still lecture while students daydream. Knowledge is still measured by tests. The administration still insists on lengthy paperwork from teachers - grades to evaluate students' work, course outlines, and objectives. Much of this is just filed and never looked at again.

The whole system is built on pretence. Administrators pretend they are very important people without whom the school would collapse. Teachers pretend to take their orders and suggestions seriously, writing out program objectives and other required statements that have little or nothing to do with actual classroom management. Students pretend to pay attention when the teachers lecture even though the information presented doesn't seem to connect to their future in any meaningful way. Most students are unable to see a relationship between school and their lives. Consequently they lose interest in learning, and if they do not drop out, then they just try to survive from report card to report card.

Unfortunately there is a lot of hypocrisy in the system which does have its devotees and a language of its own. I call the hypocrites 'educational stone heads' and the language they use 'educational B.S.'

Our universities do not prepare future teachers for the reality of the classroom either. Psychology classes do not show the enthusiastic teacher-to-be how to handle drug and suicide problems or just simply what to do when a student outright refuses to do what the teacher has instructed him to. Discipline seems to remain a cloudy issue. In our recent past, fear was what kept order. Spanking and various other punishments kept young people in line for centuries. It was effective since the order of the society was founded on fear as well. Governments ruled with terror. Religions preached punishment from the hand of a despotic God. People were commanded to live by the Ten Commandments to escape eternal Hell and to live by the rules of the government to escape jail. Fascism and Communism kept millions in a state of mindless obedience. Even now many governments use fear to stay in power.

Our freedom loving, North American society has removed rule by terror and values the rights of the individual to follow his or her personal beliefs. It is beautiful, and I am the first person to salute this, but somehow the old rules and expectations have survived in our school system. We want our students to follow our commands like soldiers. There are many rules, and the teachers are supposed to reinforce them.

Some say: "If we did not have strong regulations, then we would have anarchy." I think we can run a school with more freedom by taking into consideration individual needs and differences. For example, there is a rule: "If caught smoking, you will be suspended." Wouldn't it be better to set up a student smoking room where sympathetic teachers would sit with the kids and help them quit smoking while talking casually? Legalize anything and you take the thrill out of it.

Most students smoke because their friends, with whom they can spend time only if they prove how 'cool' they are, do. Suspension will not curtail smoking. On the contrary, students are often rather proud of being suspended. Jim walked into my class to collect his sketchbook. "I've been suspended again," he announced so everybody could hear. "Suspended, for what?" I asked. "I was caught smoking!" He walked out into the sunlight after his glorious moment of attention while the others, envying him, remained on their stools. He left in the middle of the day, and he proved himself 'cool' because he did not care. After Jim's suspension the number of kids who lit up increased,

I'm sure. Jim became a hero for a few minutes, proving how outdated the rules of the school are.

Some teenagers will experiment with alcohol, drugs, or anything else that is not allowed. The forbidden is glamorous. They want to shock their parents and teachers with their behaviour and to draw attention to themselves. Well-adjusted young people have less trouble with drugs than the neglected ones. If nobody made a fuss over drinking and smoking, fewer people would reach for cigarettes and alcohol.

My liquor cabinet at home has never been locked. I offered my children a sip of wine even when they were small. "Have a little wine. It's good for you. Red wine cures poor blood." They refused it most of the time. If I insisted, they stuck their tongue in it and made a face. Iced tea or Coke tasted better. They only drank a small glass of wine when they wanted to show off. By the time they reached the drinking age, they knew both the good and bad sides of alcohol. When at parties where other teenagers got 'smashed', they would walk away sober and disgusted by the others who had made animals out of themselves. Both of my children are moderate social drinkers who neither look upon alcohol as a means of getting high or fear it as evil.

The same thing happened with cigarettes. My son and daughter smoked for a few years, and when they did not get the hoped for attention from me, they just quit. "I am a smoker," my daughter stated recently, "who no longer lights up by choice."

Our lives are bounded by responsibilities: family, school, society, work. Some people like limits because they make them feel safe. "I know the road I will walk. My parents took the same route. Everybody goes the same way. If I do, it will be the right thing."

Others rebel, pounding against every possible fence that sets limits on their individual desires. We are all different. In school we have created the boundaries by assuming a general nature for all adolescents. Many students feel comfortable with that; some test how much they can get away with it; while a few rebel violently. This does not mean the most obedient ones are the best. Some students have natural wisdom and know where walking on the wild side would lead. Easy to discipline, also, are those who love to be told what to do. They have little imagination and don't want to make decisions on their own.

Those who struggle to test the boundaries are often kids who want to be in charge of every decision. The 'violently rebelling' ones are those attention seekers or extremely bright individuals who we can't control with rules.

The Flower brothers were good examples of opposite extremes. John had more trouble than is normal with his teachers and with his parents. He was tall and good looking, if you made the effort to look under his long hair which was brushed over one side of his face and touched the desk when he worked. Half of its length was dyed coal black, while the other half, naturally blond, made for a sharp contrast. He took two art classes but worked only when he felt like it. In the grade ten art class, he would work on his graphics projects, while in the graphics class, he would do his grade ten painting. His works were superb in quality and revealed great talent. His drawings displayed the vision of a mature artist. John was also a perfectionist who threw drawings, which I would have given good marks to but he did not find satisfactory into the garbage. Needless to say he was failing or on the verge of it in most of his other subjects because he was not willing to do projects assigned to the general student population. They did not interest or challenge his taste.

John's older brother, Ted, was one of the model students in our school. He was studious, hard working, and academically oriented, but excelled in sports, too. They were born into the same family. They grew up in the same environment, had the same upbringing and even attended the same schools. Ted was the intelligent, easily managed student; John was the one who every day challenged the teachers who made the effort to get through to him.

Ten years ago, the counsellor knocked on my door. Trailing behind him was another student - a small, black-haired Native boy with hostility and mistrust carved into his face. "Would you be kind enough to take Jerry into your art class? We can't find him an elective. Nobody wants to take him. This is the third school since September he has tried to settle into."

I looked at the little fellow and my heart went out to him. "He must be scared and lonely," I told the counsellor. "Of course I will take him."

Jerry walked into my class and immediately sat down in a corner and turned his back toward me. On his jean jacket there was a message written in felt marker: 'Fuck off'. "Oh," I thought. "If that's what you want, that's what I'll do." I left him alone for three days. He did not talk to anybody and did not touch anything. He just showed up at the starting bell, sat down, turned his back toward me and did not move until the next bell. The little fellow sat motionless, ignoring the world around him. His tiny shoulders proudly defended his inside hurt. I did not ask why he was not working. I just let him sit and wear his protective jean jacket.

The art class had just started a fabric unit, and I had brought out colourful

wools, looms, and books about weaving. Carefully, I selected most of my teaching examples from Native Indian art and introduced the students to the magic of
tapestry-making. "Well, class, here are some examples from Native artists. We
can learn from their simplicity, their excellent taste in design, and their mastery of
weaving." I told them how much I admired First Nation art and how much we,
who are all relatively new to this beautiful country that we call Canada, can learn
from their culture.

"I say this to all of you except Jerry. He already knows it because he is a proud
member of the First Nations." By this time Jerry was finally facing me and I could
see his deep dark eyes staring into mine. When I handed out the looms, I put one
in front of him, too. He picked it up and started to string it immediately. The
next day he took off his jacket, and folding it on his stool, he sat on it. There
would be no more 'Fuck off' sign for the art teacher. Jerry's back still stiffened
when I walked behind him to check his progress. It was easy to give him compli-
ments. His speedy weaving unfolded into a lovely blue, red, and white design.
He worked diligently from bell to bell until he finished with triumph.

The counsellor came again a few days later, much to my disappointment, to
take Jerry out of my class.

"He has to go. His mother died of cancer, and Jerry is moving to the island to
live on the reservation with his grandparents."

The little fellow stood there with his jacket folded under his arm. I put his
weaving in his hand.

"I am sorry you're leaving us. You are quite an artist. I gave you an A on this
project."

He took it, then looked down at the floor and then up at me again.

"I made it for my Mom," he said, "but I have no use for it anymore, I guess.
You can have it if you want it." That was his first and last sentence. I held the
little weaving to my heart and thanked him while swallowing my tears.

Jerry left the school and I never saw him again, but I often think of him when
I show his work to students as an example during weaving classes every year. I
hope he found the noble warrior he is inside. Instead of building more barriers
to shelter himself from further hurt, I hope he used his splendid Indian heritage
to enrich our multicultural tapestry.

Freedom - that is what Canadian society and our Charter of Rights stand for.

But it is not easy to live in a free society. Some people find it hard to handle. Being free means they have to make their own choices and with that there always comes the possibility of picking wrong. Parents wish they could save their children from their own mistakes. But can they?

Would it lead to anarchy if we let our young ones choose what to do or not to do? Do we adequately prepare our children for life if we make their decisions for them and expect them to obey without question? Do you want them always to do what they have been told?

I have found that teenagers can pretty well find what is right and wrong without rigid rules. If you treat them with respect, they respond with respect. If you show a genuine interest in their affairs, they are honest in return. If you believe in their ability to do something, they try to show their best. If you show them love, they love you back.

At the beginning of the year, I put an effort into making my students understand that we do not have rules in the art room. Rules are made for herds of sheep, not for intelligent human beings. My rights and wrongs are not necessarily theirs. If they do not understand the reasons I expect certain behaviour of them, I am willing to listen and debate. I urge them to challenge me. I am older and have more experience. They are young and have a fresh outlook on life. I counsel my students to tell me if they do not agree and to stand up for themselves. I am there to help and guide, and I am their friend. All I expect is that they will be as fair with me as I am with them.

Most teenagers go into a state of shock when they see I will let them to explore to see whether I meant what I said or if it was just empty talk. Nobody can teach a child against his will. I strongly agree with Albert Einstein when he said: "I never teach my pupils. I only attempt to provide the conditions in which they learn."

Through a trial and error period at the beginning of each semester, my students learn to clean up, to respect other people's property, to tolerate differing opinions, and to forgive. Without these disciplines, no creative work can be done. They call learning in my room fun instead of work, and when they enjoy what they do, they learn not just to paint or draw creatively, but also gain social skills, self-worth and self-expression.

At the end of the year I always ask "What did you learn from your art class this year?" A rough-looking fifteen year old boy once answered this way: "I learned it is possible to love everybody."

•••
CHAPTER XXIV
•••

I should no longer have to convince anyone who has read my story thus far of my dedication for teaching. However, my love affair with education has not made the job perfect by any means. Some days I start with enthusiasm and finish with frustration. I must confess that there have been many days when I closed the doors after the last student and went around kicking the garbage cans as an outlet for my anger. Many times I have sat in my car for five or ten minutes before driving home waiting for my hands to stop shaking or my tears to relieve the built-up frustration.

Public schools are big pots filled with a stew that combines a great variety of people. Well-disciplined, hard-working students mix with pot smokers; lazy ones mingle with youngsters who think that violence is cool and that the more pushy you are, the more manly you prove yourself. Quiet or shy kids with average ability are caught between the high achievers and the rowdy ones. The students come from different family, racial, and religious backgrounds and values. Still the education system tries to push everybody through the same grinder before they enter the world.

We should all be asking the question: how relevant is the curriculum to the lives of our students?

Tracy was in grade ten. She had a natural talent in graphic art. She used the imagery of graphic communication with ease. Her posters delivered her messages in simple and striking ways. She took two art classes and tried to slip into the others as a way of escaping Mathematics sessions. Consequently, she was failing Math 10 and had A's in both art classes. Her bright, beautiful eyes filled up with tears when I tried to send her back to Math, so we sat down for a lengthy talk after school. I told her she must cope with Math if she wanted to enter college. Otherwise she would block her path to higher education. Should a student or the system be blamed for failing when such a tortured effort is required from someone whose right brain is far more developed than the left?

I asked my friend Jerry, a dedicated teacher who spends four nights out of five in the school helping students lost in Math, to give Tracy a hand. He did help willingly. But in the age of the sophisticated calculators why should Jerry have to spend ten to fifteen extra hours without pay to teach a student whose brain stops functioning when it comes to numbers?

Holding Tracy with one hand and wiping her tears with the other, I thought back thirty years. My own Mathematics tests and exams gave me countless sleepless nights as a teenager. I have never used what I sweated so hard to learn. I still dream about sitting at my school desk, staring at the paper with a panicky feeling in my stomach. "Why do I have to write the test? I am already a teacher?" Then I wake up in relief to find it was only a dream. All the Math I have needed throughout my life I had already learned in elementary school. The rest of the time was wasted.

When is the education system going to change to allow students with artistic ability to pursue their interests and still be eligible for a post secondary education in college or university? There is a strong trend toward requiring art courses for high school graduation. The United States where twenty states have added Art to their requirements since 1980 is ahead of Canada. Here I quote Ernest Boyes: "The arts are the means by which civilization can be measured . . . they are not a frill. We recommend that all students study the arts. These skills are no longer just desirable. They are essential if we are to survive together with civility and joy."

Our school system expects young ones to sit through four to five classes daily listening to lecturers. Honestly, how many in a class of thirty hear - really hear - what the teacher talks about? People do not like to listen. They mostly like to be heard. You can prepare the most interesting topic and present it with enthusiasm, but after three to five minutes you will lose two-thirds of your audience unless you involve them. Good teachers ask questions and let the students arrive at their own conclusions. Master teachers make the students participate in everything. They inspire creative thinking by grouping the students to solve both practical and theoretical problems. Regardless of the subject you teach, there is no justification for handing down information that seems to be irrelevant to the student's everyday life and then expect them to retain it.

Forcing students to practise mindless memorization was one of the mistakes of the past and it still haunts students when they must prepare for a test today. Lots of students dislike Social Studies classes because they are expected to learn names and dates and colour countless maps. History and geography could be the most exciting of subjects if only teachers presented the material in the form of interesting stories relevant to students' present lives.

The introduction of the Western Civilization course in grade twelve was a success. Why? Because Kenneth Clark used the history of art as a way to get people to reflect on their present civilization. Many students have confessed that they only began to understand history when they attended the Western Civilization course. Looking at the creations of the human race - from cave paintings to Modern art - suddenly made those thousands of years of history comprehensible. In a way facts and meaningless names and numbers cannot, the masterpieces of the world reach out and touch the heart of the present generation. The artists' hopes and dreams, their suffering and successes, are communicated through their visual images to our young people. Emotions thus communicated awaken thought, and when students start to think instead of just memorizing, we can be assured that they have gained knowledge and not just passed a test.

A good teacher never 'teaches'. 'Teaching' is too close to the word 'preaching'. Students only learn when they are interested, so the teacher's speeches should be short like dropping a stone into water. A teacher must then step aside to give the students the opportunity to think to form the ripples in the water thereafter. Their first question is always: "Why do we have to learn this? What is the use of this exercise?" If a teacher can't come up with a legitimate answer, he might as well throw the lesson plan into the waste basket. A good teacher is only a guide who presents a smorgasbord of knowledge for students to choose from. Nobody can be forced to learn. Motivation is the key.

Far too many subjects emphasize mindless repetition of the facts. Learning only the names of the rivers and the mountains will not teach students about our planet or about the exciting variety of its landscapes and the flesh-and-blood people who inhabit them. Similarly, testing recall of factual knowledge has very little if any value. Most students prepare for exams by cramming information into their short term memories. Just question the best students who achieve A's three days after a test. Only one out of ten will be able recall the details studied. Very few people have the ability to store facts. I call those who can 'lexicon brains'. Most of us are unable to do that.

I do not want to say facts are unimportant, but they should mainly be stored away for further reference. For centuries that purpose has been well served by libraries, and now in the computer age, we have a great tool for people who have a visual type of memory.

The success of the future generation is dependent upon creative thinking. It is invaluable and absolutely essential. Get students involved; let them talk. While they put their thoughts into sentences, they learn more about a subject than any teacher can achieve with the most well-prepared lecture. With independent thinking, encouraged students gain a wider perspective of the presented topic. The awakened thoughts trigger actions, and actions bring about change.

Adolescence is a stage of discovery. Teenagers try to find out who they are and what the world around them is like. In school they are only interested in material that seems to relate directly to their lives. It is the teacher's responsibility to make the subject matter relevant and to help children discover. Self-discovery should be the most important activity in every school. Self-expression can be best learned through a variety of arts - language, visual, music, drama, and movement.

Subjects offered in the traditional way, separate from one another, are like building materials - lumber, brick, glass or concrete. They have the possibility of becoming a house, but only become useful when a builder puts them together. Similarly, the integration of subjects in school would bring the curriculum to life. I have been teaching art for sixteen years without really knowing what my students are learning in English, Science or History in the same year.

There are a few visionary teachers who, in partnership, make their lessons parallel, providing their students many views of the same themes and events. I work with the E.S.L. (English as a Second Language) teacher in our school to encourage an understanding through art of the wide diversity of our students' cultural heritages. Would it not be excellent if P.E. teachers offered Greek folk dance or discussed the meaning of the Olympic Games with their classes while math classes discussed Pythagoras. At the same time the drama department had students practice public speaking and the Social Studies people showed slides or videos about Greece while in the art room students decorated their clay pots with Greek designs? The possibilities for overlapping instruction like this are endless. By joining subjects in this way they become relevant to one another and thus come to life. Students are more likely to see history's value when it becomes something tangible.

In some places there is a tendency to end the segregation of learning and to remove the classroom walls allowing the students to explore the whole of knowledge instead of just the parts. The Jason Project is one example. It uses advanced technology to bring the outside world and its excitement right into the classroom by transmitting via satellite images of exploration taking place on the bottom of the Mediterranean ocean. If only teachers were willing to put aside their dusty files of old lesson plans and attempt new ways of reaching students. I hope this is what is going to happen in education. Visionary teachers do that already.

Learning facts engages only a portion of the intellectual mind. To be able to apply knowledge to solve present day issues of society and the world is the key to responsible and aware personhood. By putting greater emphasis on present day knowledge to come, the imagination combined with knowledge of the past will enable the capable intellect of the future.

Unfortunately, our society still does not put enough emphasis on the arts. Math and Science are mandatory subjects whereas the arts are only electives in our school system. Art classes are often regarded as less serious than academics. Even teachers think of art as some easy-to-teach subject not essential for a young person to graduate into life. In academic subjects schools offer regular, enriched and fundamentals classes. Only in electives like the arts are the outstanding students mixed with the slower learners and the motivated are thrown together with the uninterested. Dedicated teachers put a tremendous effort into motivating the lazy ones and challenging the talented ones at the same time. These teachers play multiple roles every day in every class. They become actors, counsellors, lecturers, mothers and artists depending on the needs of any given moment.

I consider myself a guide or a facilitator in class, not an authority figure. I expect as much respect and love from my pupils as I give. I truly believe that every person has talent in some area and it is my challenge to discover where that talent lies.

I believe in the public school system. Private schools isolate their students even more from society. Young people there often start to believe they are more special than the rest of their peers who attend mass education programs.

The future is in the hands of the many, not only the privileged few. The millions of young people all over the world who are now spending their most difficult years from thirteen to sixteen in the public school system will determine our future. Change is needed for them. Let's throw away our hypocrisy and take an honest look at our education system. We must stop hiding behind big words of our educational B.S. and finally admit that our system is far from perfect, and that not all teachers are dedicated. We teachers have to learn to change constantly so we'll be able to prepare our youth for the future.

New technologies like computers, videos, and satellite dishes are forcing the roles a teacher plays to change, too. The pre-conceived notion of a teacher as someone who knows everything is a fallacy. Our role is becoming that of a guide for the new generation while they pursue their search for identity and for their place in society. We have to create in our schools person-to-person relationships between teachers and students to ensure a productive atmosphere and to avoid wasting more time in maintaining the false authoritarian atmosphere.

The revolutionary overthrow of the old education system is already brewing. Many articles are being written about this. Already new concepts of what is really important like global thinking, environmental concerns are finding their way into our school programs. The old system is crumbling, and the new is struggling to be born. For example, the birth of global education which means teaching with a global perspective.

Many teachers are frightened of the coming changes. They say it is too much, too fast. But an equal number of humane, caring educators welcome the transformation and can't get far enough along fast enough. Unfortunately, this means while the debate is ongoing that educational institutions will be first pulled back and then pushed forward by opposing forces, while the kids caught inside continue to lose out.

•••

CHAPTER XXV

•••

Teenagers with low self esteem are the ones whose behaviour becomes hostile, rowdy, or violent. These troubled young people are labelled by parents, teachers, and society as stupid, incapable, and good for nothing. Their defence is either to withdraw or to gang up with other youngsters who have similar problems and distrust everything that comes from authority figures.

Even those teenagers who grow up in a loving and supporting environment will have an identity crisis between the ages of thirteen and sixteen. Those years of transition from childhood to adulthood take a toll on every individual, but imagine the hardships suffered when loving support is lacking.

Many students come to school from a home where the Mother lives with a boyfriend or Dad has a girlfriend or the parents are together but constantly fighting. These adults are pre-occupied with the problems of their own relationships and have little time for their offspring. They send them to school to be taken care of and then get upset when their teenagers act up. After all, haven't they provided food, shelter, and a comfortable life for the kids? Shouldn't their children be grateful enough not to fail subjects and get into trouble?

Quarrelling with teenagers never improves the situation. They need to be told often that they are valuable and precious beings, and to have the good in them pointed out constantly. Every human has something unique and good to offer. Parents who focus on the positive while giving guidance, will improve their children's self-image.

Far too many times I have heard the following statement: "I won't try that because I am stupid." That always makes me sad.

"What do you mean you are stupid?"

"Oh, my mother says it too. Everybody knows. I'm failing everything."

This is when I must sit down at the student's work table and look straight into his eyes.

"That's everybody except me. I know you are intelligent. You are you! Do not compare yourself to anybody else. Straight A's do not make a person smarter or any more valuable. Don't you know that Einstein failed in school? Wasn't he a genius? Just look at yourself. You are young with your whole life ahead of you. You are healthy and good-looking, too. You must have a special talent - something that you can do best. Everybody has. Discover it and use it." Then I ask the student what he likes to do, what he is most interested in, and what he plans to do with his life?

A few days later, I make sure to find in that person's art project something interesting, unique, or nice and to praise him in front of the class. Lots of drawings appear on my display board that make others wonder why they got there. I know the answer when the artists who drew them bring their friends at lunch time to show off their displayed works.

Have you ever wondered how some of the modern sculptures or paintings made it into the galleries? What does a seemingly chaotic mass of wire, glass or paint express? Certainly not beauty, order, or classical values. Learning about the personal experiences and feelings of an artist can make the message he wants to deliver through his artwork understandable.

It is heartbreaking to see the number of art projects in high school that express confusion, loneliness, hurt, and feelings of being lost. One of the most successful projects I do with my grade nines is the self-portrait. Students are asked not to draw what they look like but the way they feel inside. Expressing emotions with colours, lines and shapes provides those who have no drawing skills a way to be successful. Few teenagers use bright colours, and many of them draw tangled dark lines or a tiny, crouched body hidden in one corner of the page.

Teenagers who walk on the edge need more attention and love than the more balanced ones. I find myself spending much more time with those who are struggling with their identity and have poor self-images. They are the students who are more likely to act out and create problems. Instead of punishing them, I discipline with love only.

Showing a genuine interest in their lives and affairs and being sensitive towards their feelings gives me better class control than the traditional 'iron grip' method. The expression 'class control' means to me providing an environment in which young people enjoy what they are doing and consequently really learn.

One day the vice principal visited the clay room where the students and I were up to our elbows in wet mud. A ghetto blaster set at high volume tried to overpower the noise from the pottery wheels and the happy chit-chat of the students.

He looked a bit shocked and advised me to use my prep period to visit the class of a teacher he felt had 'perfect class management'.

So I did. Total silence met me when I stepped into the other teacher's room. Her chalk writing on the blackboard sounded loud. The kids were sitting, frozen motionless, in their desks. One of them raised his hand to ask permission to sharpen his pencil. The teacher lectured in a low key, monotonous voice. She did not have to raise her voice to get the attention of her students. "Gee," I thought, "I sometimes have to tell jokes or say something funny or outrageous to attain complete silence in my room." After five minutes, the woman's voice seemed to disappear and I found myself daydreaming. When she asked questions, a few hands went up. I suspected they belonged to those who study and listen diligently in any situation. I looked at a few students who are very much alive when they are in my art room; here their eyes looked blank and lifeless. At the end of the period I congratulated the teacher for her fantastic class control. "How are you able to maintain that?" I asked. "Oh, it's easy," she said. "If somebody misbehaves I give the person detention, or a hundred lines to write, or deduct points from their grades. They know I am persistent and they can't get away with anything."

I thought about a black grade eight student whose big dark eyes expressed so much life when he would bang on an art room table top with his skinny arms using it as a drum to get the African rhythm out of his system before he settled down to draw for fifteen minutes. Shortly after, he'd jump up again and dance wildly between the tables, clapping his hands and blowing through his lips for music. "Do-do-do-toa-ta-ta-brums!" It delighted me. Then he would sit down again for another ten minutes of concentrated drawing.

The next period back in my classroom I asked one of my students from the other woman's class, "What she was talking about today?"

The kid wondered if I was serious. "I don't know Ms. H. I never pay any attention."

"Don't say that. You were an angel in her class, but you're a little devil in mine."

"That's different, Ms. H. That old bag punishes us, so I pretend to listen, but I really do listen when you talk, even if I'm not sitting silently."

"What do you mean? How can she be an old bag? She's at least twenty years younger than I am. What do you call me then?"

"Nothing, we love you. You're not old. You fit right in with us." I get lots of love from my students. They find it hard to be rude when I hold my arms open for them.

One day I listened to a C.B.C. radio reporter interviewing Shirley MacLaine. "What is your concept of evil?" he asked.

"Lack of enlightenment, lack of light, lack of God, total absence of love, and zero self-esteem," was her answer.

Three cheers for Shirley MacLaine. She could not say anything I agree with more. All the problems society and parents have with teenagers can be traced back to the "absence of love and zero self-esteem." At sometime during the upbringing of the child there must have been conditioning in unworthiness. If the child is lucky enough to find a person, a friend, a teacher, a nurse, or a priest who gives him respect and recognition, he will remain devoted to that person for a lifetime.

I think this is the time to tell the story of little Susan.

She showed up in the art room twelve years ago - a skinny, flat-chested blond kid with huge grey eyes staring out of a tiny freckled face. For a while until I learned all the names in the class, I thought she was a boy.

Little Susan attended more art classes than she was timetabled into. She was not alone in this. Many students skip other subjects to attend my classes. Sometimes it takes me a while to discover that Paul or John was in for the second time on a given day. Because most of my classes are overcrowded, I use an informal seating arrangement and I am a little 'loose' with my attendance taking. I have difficulty remembering to check the register when thirty or more students pour through the door every hour and I'm trying to get them all involved with paint and brushes, scissors and glue, or clay and glazes.

Susan loved the clay unit the most. She was totally absorbed while moulding the clay into human or animal figures. Her most successful work depicted a teen- ager dressed in blue jeans and a torn T-shirt holding her right hand forward. The middle finger of the exaggerated hand was extended straight up into the face of whoever looked at the sculpture.

"How do you like it?" she asked with some uncertainty in her voice. I looked at the skinny little girl with her honest creation and declared: "It is excellent, Susan. Art is self-expression and I see you are trying to tell the world what you think of it." A golden smile of great relief showed on her face.

Two months later, Susan come to say goodbye. She had to move back with her parents in Williams Lake. "I will miss you, Susan," I told her from my heart. "Me, too," she replied. "Will you give me your phone number and your address please! I will write and phone, too." she said. I jotted these down on a piece of paper and handed it over thinking I would probably never hear from her again.

I was wrong. Susan wrote two or three times a year, and sometimes even phoned, so I was kept up to date about her life and her family. Her sister got pregnant. The family got a new dog. I heard how the teachers conducted their classes in her school, and eventually why and how she dropped out before finishing.

One day she phoned. "I'm in trouble, Ms. H. I'm most likely going to end up in prison."

"But why, Susan?"

"Drugs, Ms. H." was her too short answer. I fell silent. I did not ask her how she could have done that; rather I told her I cared about her regardless of how it turned out.

Next she phoned from the prison and asked me to visit. A year later when she got out, she visited me bringing along a photo album that recorded her prison life in pictures. I learned about her cell mates and life behind bars. She had painted a mural on the wall of her cell. The photographs showed a winged unicorn flying high in the blue clouds. The unicorn earned not only my appreciation, but that of the prison guards as well. Susan's next assignment had been a wall mural in the community room.

After serving her time she did not move back to Williams Lake. She rented a romantic shack on the outskirts of Vancouver. I was invited one day for lunch to meet her roommate, a divorced woman in her late twenties whose two children were in the custody of their father. She was alone, too, and desperately trying to scrape together her shattered life.

Half a year later, Susan visited me at school bringing the happy news that she was pregnant. When I inquired about her plans regarding the pregnancy, she looked at me with surprise: "But of course, I am going to have the baby!" Living on social assistance and having a baby without a father did not seem to me much reason to be happy, but I was wrong.

The next time Susan phoned me it was from the hospital. "I am here in the maternity ward, and I have labour pains." There was a little fear underlying her voice.

"It is wonderful," I said. "There's nothing to those pains. They come and go. Just keep thinking that soon you're going to hug your own child." She did. A healthy boy was born. He inherited his mother's tiny face and huge saucer eyes. Last summer, when I visited them, the little fellow was three years of age and knew all the numbers from zero to ten and also the letters of the alphabet. To my surprise, he brought the magnetic letters and numbers from the fridge door in the order I asked for them. He was better at his letters than some of my grade nines who have difficulty reading and writing at the age of fourteen. His father, a Greek man, sometimes visited him, so the bright little fellow had picked up quite a vocabulary of Greek words, too.

The last time Susan phoned, they were packing to leave for a year in Greece. "Goodbye, Ms. H. I will write." A month later her first postcard arrived. The blue and white landscape of the card matched the mood of her writing - optimism for their future beside the azure water of the Mediterranean Sea. "I will do my art here. I might even sell it. Do not worry about me and my son, Ms. H."

No, I don't worry. I keep my hopes high and my fingers crossed for Susan and her little scholar. Dropping out of school, messing with drugs, sitting behind bars, having an illegitimate son - Susan, you are a beautiful person. You just chose to walk on the 'wild side' as your way of learning life's lessons. God help you to achieve self-acceptance, self-esteem, and love.

'Bad' experiences can be a very effective way for a person to learn, provided he is not forever crippled by guilt. Guilt and a bad conscience often arise from failing the expectations of one's family or society's standards. I don't think Susan has to worry about that. She showed more than enough bravery in grade eight when she created her clay figure that gave the world the finger.

•••
CHAPTER XXVI
•••

"I wish teachers weren't prejudiced against certain students. They should see them for the way they express themselves in their work, not how they express themselves in their dress or talk." This is a quotation from Michelle, a grade ten student.

"I think that teachers should end their hypocrisy and stop abusing their right to punish students and tell them what to do. Schools should cater to the needs of students. I think that school is also too boring. It should be built around feelings of growing up and other aspects of human psyche." This quotation comes from John, also a grade ten student.

Children are people just like grown-ups are. Good-willed or bad-willed, smart, slow, talented, afraid to use their resources - these qualities do not come with being a certain age. You can find extremely wise eight year olds and fifty year olds who limit the potential of their thinking.

Who determines when a child becomes a full person? Does it happen overnight at the age of sixteen when she can drive or nineteen when he can drink and vote?

During my long years of teaching, I have met some students who were wiser than some of my university professors and others who were as limited in their capacity for self-expression as my bunny rabbit.

Every child has full human potential inside because every person has a brain far more sophisticated than the most advanced computer. The problem lies in our limited ability to switch that brain on and use it to its maximum potential. The basic requirement to meet this goal is having a loving, understanding, tolerant, non-judgemental, and accepting environment at home and at school.

Most of the students who do well in school come from caring, loving homes. Those who are trouble-makers not always but often come from families who lack the above qualities. In public schools, the student population is recruited from all kind of backgrounds. There is not much the system can do to correct all the mistakes that parents make. However, providing more courses focused on self-discovery, self-acceptance, or as John put it on "feelings" and the problems of "growing up," would build a new generation who, by the time they became parents, could do a much better job of guiding their own children.

Fear is the most crippling factor in human growth. A loving and safe environment makes the child free to express his or her personality. What a difference it makes when a child learns it is O.K. to make mistakes because everybody does! Mistakes are excellent tools of learning. Is it more valuable for a person to avoid wrong-doing out of the fear of punishment from parents, teachers or authorities or to avoid it because he has tried it and the outcome proved to him the futility of negative actions? Teenagers who have never tried adventures are not necessarily good. People gain knowledge from their experiences and sometimes a walk on the 'wild side' will make that human being better than one who is afraid to venture into areas considered 'bad' according to the general morals of society.

I do not suggest that this is the only way to learn what is good or bad in life. Most people don't have to steal, cheat, or lie to know that these things do not pay in the long run. However, we all know people who have become bitter as they grew older. They are jealous of the younger generation because they feel they missed out. They were reluctant to try things in their youth and so denied themselves certain experiences fearing their parents, God's punishment or what other people think of them. Who has not had an aunt or other older family member look at us with strong disapproval when we were young and wild? Many of us carry the memory of her piercing eyes and tightly closed narrow lips surrounded with tiny lines - the bitterness etched deep in her face as she passed judgement on our behaviour from her ivory tower of strong morality.

How different it is to be looked at by someone with an accepting sparkle in the eye and an understanding smile. Only these open people are able to truly communicate with youth and lend a helping hand when it is needed.

I accept all my students as they are, respect their personal differences, and try to make them understand I really do care. My genuine interest in people makes it surprisingly easy for me to communicate with adolescents. Seeking advice, help, or just in need of a sympathetic ear, they tell me about their problems and their affairs openly.

Mike and Mike had been friends since elementary school. They signed up for classes together and tried to keep their lives parallel in every way they could. Both of them came from families where no books or magazines lay on the tables. In both families the parents made an honest living from manual work. Consequently, the two Mikes did not see any point to studying academic subjects. They enjoyed sports, woodwork classes, and battled their way through grade eight. But by grade nine, they were failing most of the mandatory subjects. They did not pay attention to lectures. They daydreamed about driving hot cars, dating girls, and getting drunk. A person can't spend three or four hours a day fantasizing, so they created some excitement by skipping classes, smoking in the washroom, and planting stink bombs in the hallway garbage cans. They spent considerable time in the vice principal's office and at home whenever they'd been suspended, which was often.

Both Mikes were assigned to my home room when they finally reached grade ten. I still can see them in my memory - the blond hair of one straight and the other as curly as a Murillo angel. With their bright blue eyes and muscular, stocky bodies, they could have been brothers.

These boys needed my help frequently. I would give them late slips and talk to their subject teachers, trying to postpone the inevitable day when they would be expelled. I loved those two capable young teenagers, who were discarded and lost by our educational system. Half way through grade ten, they had to leave for good. Did they fail us, or did our school fail them? I think it was the latter.

By the time they had reached grade ten, they were convinced of their inability to learn. They thought of themselves as trouble makers. After all they had been told many times by their parents, by the vice principal, and by the teachers that they were just that. During the last confrontation, one of them punched the principal. They came to tell me the story and to say good bye.

"We love you, Ms. H." they said. "We'll come back to visit you one day," they promised, and they did. Two weeks later, when the final bell of the day rang, the two Mikes walked into the school with a bottle of champagne in hand and made their way up to the art room.

The principal saw this through his window and ran after them together with the vice principal. I was tidying up after my last class when Mike and Mike appeared and gave me their present. I put the bottle on my desk and hugged the two boys wishing them well when suddenly both of my doors flew open and the principal and vice principal bolted into the room. They stopped dead at the sight of us hugging. I can honestly say that it was one of the most uncomfortable moments of my teaching career.

At the time our school had a principal who had communication problems not just with students, but with the teachers as well. His rigid, strong arm approach to everything had made the staff bitter and even hostile. We had taken votes of non-confidence and had asked him to resign many times. The school board had a growing file of complaints from his staff. Still it was many years before he finally moved. He was not a bad person - just incapable of handling his job.

Now all of this happened in the past. That principal and the two blond-haired Mikes were just memories, until a few days ago, when somebody came into the art room and covered my eyes from behind. I reached for the hands and turned around to see a suntanned face, bright blue eyes, and the light, curly hair of one Mike. He wrapped his arm around me giving me a bear hug and a big kiss on the cheek. My grade eight class watched with interest. "Hi, Ms. H., do you remember of me?" "Of course, my son, how are you?" "I'm fine. I came to tell you that I bought a truck and now make good money. My girlfriend is in your grade ten home room, just like I was six years ago. I'm happy."

So was I. After Mike's report on his life, I turned my attention back to the class. They no longer asked me if visitors who came were my son or daughter. They had gotten used to seeing people drop in. Few days pass without an ex-student coming to see me. They come to tell about their lives, weddings, and new jobs and to bring their newborn infants in for me to see. All the love and care I gave out is coming back a hundredfold. This makes me feel very proud and successful. After all, I touched their hearts and taught them as they drew and painted that there is something more important than any school subject. That is the value of human relationships. There are people out there who care for each other. We are not alone.

I know my teaching is unconventional. I do not claim my way is the only way to relate to teenagers, but what I have presented here works for me.

"How do you discipline those awful teenagers?" somebody once asked me. "I love them. That is the method I use for discipline." That statement has raised quite a few eyebrows.

Adults do discriminate against children, especially teenagers, the same way as some people still discriminate against different races. I do not advise all teachers to hug their students or get involved in their personal lives, but I believe in the following:

Treat your child or your students as you do fully grown people. Perhaps the experiences of the young are limited compared to ours, but their lack of experience sometimes means a lack of brain washing. We older people are conditioned more or less by social and religious beliefs to accept the standards of society even though the rules sometimes seem senseless.

Guide with your knowledge. Do not say your way is the only way to go. Give your advice with the option of accepting or rejecting it. Let the young listener make his own decision. If the road he takes leads to trouble, do not say: "See, I told you so!" Rather say: "Regardless of your choice, I am here to help you. You can count on my support as a parent or as a teacher, because I care."

Turning against your teenager, just because he made a bad choice, will not teach the young one respect. He will decide you do not understand him. If anything, that will make him more stubborn and push him into deeper trouble. He will build a wall to keep you out and to protect himself. He will start to pretend or lie to keep you off his back. In other words, communication will entirely break down.

It is worth keeping your doors open. Listen to your teenager! They have a fresh outlook on life. Sometimes they are the ones who are right. We who have walked thirty or more years since we were teenagers often lose the vision of the child inside. It gets buried under common beliefs and outdated morals that society has imposed on us through schooling, the media, and religion. What we may need is a good mental house cleaning or a re-evaluation of the old values.

Is our success in life measured by the pay cheques we receive, the house we have, or the car we drive? How many of us still know how to play? I don't mean how to play tennis or card games, but truly amuse ourselves as we used to in childhood? How many of us still like to climb trees or skip flat stones across the surface of a pond? How many of us take off our shoes to stamp in the puddles after a summer rain or roll in a pile of autumn leaves. When did you last roll down a grassy hill?

Are you afraid you'll lose respect if you play fight with your child, wrestling, pinching, and laughing? Have you ever sat down to listen to your teenager's favourite band and tried to understand the text of the songs? Did you ever go to a rock concert with your child? Or are you the type who declares the tapes they listen to are noise and not music? Can you talk to your teen about your hopes, your dreams, and your failures? Have you ever talked honestly with your kid about sex?

This list can go on and on. The idea is for you to take an interest in the affairs of your teenager. Don't watch over their activities from up high with authoritarian eyes, but take part in them. Mingle with your children and their friends. You will be surprised how readily they take you in and how proudly your teenager will tell his friends: "This is my Mom, who is really great because she understands."

There is only one measure by which to decide what is good and what is bad. What leads to fear is bad, what leads to love is good. If you don't know how to handle a situation, how to advise your growing children, just listen to your heart. Any action that will create fear is wrong, and all the actions that increase the love between you and your teenager are good. I believe in this and live by it. It has worked for me and I suggest you give it a try yourself.

CHAPTER XXVII

Vancouver is a gateway city and a harbour city. A reception centre for people from the East, its population is truly multicultural. In our workplaces, colleagues from around the globe mix. We can dine on cuisine from all over the world just by walking down any of the major streets. Our children grow up sharing classes with the offspring of Native, Japanese, Chinese, Vietnamese, African, Latin American and European families. Almost every country is represented in our schools.

At the beginning of the year when I greet my new students, freshly washed faces of all colours look up at me. Needless to say, I welcome the multicultural nature of my class with happiness in my heart. The future of the world depends on the spirit of internationalism and global awareness. The borders between nations, created by chauvinistic and nationalistic thinking, must come down. In the future, I hope every person will realize that we are all fellow travellers on this earth. We must join hands and give our best to build a better world where no war, discrimination, or hatred exists.

Unfortunately, not everybody thinks in global terms. Some of our students come from families where parents talk with prejudice, labelling people with such phrases as: "Lazy Indian, stinking Punjabi, stupid Chinaman." It is hard to educate against discrimination when that kind of tone has been set in the home.

Our schools are trying hard to teach young people to treat everybody as equals. For example, we have organized an International Club that puts on displays from different cultures, hosts guest speakers, and organizes programs featuring international folk dances. Through performing and visual arts, through lectures and videos, schools are trying to raise the awareness of the new generation and increase their knowledge of the thousands of years of heritage of Native, Asian, African, Latin American and European people.

Needless to say, many honour roll students in schools now have Chinese or Japanese backgrounds or come from newly arrived European families. Why do they excel and why are the second or third generation Canadians failing? Immigrant families work hard to build a new life in a new country. These kids grow up with parents who do not spare themselves when it comes to hard work and have a different outlook on life from people who've always lived in comfort and see little incentive to try for more.

Laziness seems to be the sickness of North American youth. Their lives are too easy - with no hardships and everything provided for them, they take 'the good life' for granted. This shows in the way they carelessly waste paper and the way they crush soft drink cans and throw them onto the floor instead of returning them for the five cent deposit. At lunch time, countless numbers of uneaten sandwiches end up in the garbage or are thrown on the floor. Kids want to buy potato chips or MacDonald's hamburgers instead.

Two of my top art students, Wayne and Frank came from an immigrant family. Their hands were rough and covered with scratches when they first picked up a brush in September to create the most astonishingly beautiful paintings. I found out that they had worked throughout the summer picking berries from sunrise to sunset, seven days a week. This labour out in the burning sun had earned them thirty or forty dollars a day, which was all handed over to their parents to contribute to living expenses. I asked some other students who complained about their lack of money why they didn't try picking berries? Most of them looked me with horror: "You must be kidding, Ms. H. That's for Hindus. I am not going to mix with them!" Whose fault is it that they think this way? Do we blame the young people themselves, or their parents, or society?

I do not suggest all parents should send their teenage children out into the berry fields, but I definitely advise everyone to encourage greater responsibility by arranging jobs for teens during the summer holidays. Teach your children to respect all kinds of labour and to value money earned by working.

Most households in North America throw away food that would go a long way towards feeding families in the developing world. Waste, waste and more waste is what growing children see all around them. This ranges from the endless piles of advertising pamphlets thrown on our doorsteps every day to the grass clippings and raked leaves left in green bags for garbage collection instead of being composted and recycled.

Teaching young ones to value everything that nature provides - fresh air, clean water, and good food - would create a better society. This education must start at home with the parents leading by example. Environmental awareness is the foundation for a better future.

When I slice a loaf of bread I collect the crumbs and put them into the dog dish. The post-war years taught me to value food. The smashed sandwiches and the apples and oranges thrown away every lunch period make me feel sick at heart. When I speak against such needless waste, the students look at me without comprehending my words.

All schools should start recycling programs. It may sound extreme, but one way would be to keep pigs in the back schoolyard to consume the discarded food. Schools could reserve a piece of land from the large playing fields for cultivating vegetables. We could make it part of Home Economics classes to teach children how to plant, fertilize, weed, and harvest vegetables. Country children have the opportunity to learn these skills at home, but what about the city kids? That kind of knowledge could save their lives in the twenty-first century, when 'going green' or dying might be the only choices they have. All Social Studies and Science classes should teach an appreciation of natural resources and environmental protection, instead of just giving children numbers and names to memorize and then forget after tests have been written.

If we taught our children what Native people have known for thousands of years - namely that we are not the masters of Nature, but a small part of it, and so are equal to all living things, plants and animals and even the rocks and soil – then, when grown, they would stop the multi-million dollar corporations from polluting the earth, destroying the ozone layer, and spilling deadly oil into the oceans. I think we are living in the eleventh hour. There is still time to save the world from destroying all its God-given wealth and restore the ecological balance but not much.

Is our society doing everything it can to educate the young generation to be aware of this? As parents, do we model through our household management our concern for the environment by doing everything we can not to pollute the water or the air and not to waste food and recycle everything we possibly can? I do not mean we should scare children and generate fear. I want them to learn to show respect and love toward all things on the Earth that support our life. We must teach this by modelling loving care.

Not long ago, when the danger of nuclear war was more pressing, students expressed so much fear in their writing and drawings, it was almost crippling.

"What is the use of studying? What is the use of trying? We might as well live it up while we can." The possibility of nuclear devastation still haunts our youth. "Draw a picture illustrating life in 2100 as you imagine it." In a class of thirty, at least ten will hand in barren landscapes with scattered skyscrapers and skeletons on the ground. Television is a powerful force that helps amplify this fear. Children now can watch large oil spills killing the sea mammals and birds, polluted lakes with thousands of dead fish washing ashore, or millions of people starving in Africa. We have earthquake drills in school, and reported by the media, scientists predict devastating earthquakes will come during our lifetime. Fear, fear, and fear!

What messages do teenagers get from all of this? The world is a hostile place. The future is uncertain. They feel powerless in the face of all the possible horrors that may come. What can a single person do against all that? Can parents or the government offer protection? It seems very unlikely to our children, so they say: "Let's get the most out of the present. Party! Live it up!"

Planting fear in the hearts of children is the worst thing we can do. If we hopelessly expect the worst, that is what will happen. We must teach positive thinking at home, at school, and through television and newspapers. Instead of focusing on horror stories, we should highlight the actions of everyone who tries to make the world a better place.

The only way to change the world is to start with yourself. All people are equally important. Every person counts. We can save the world with a new generation that thinks positively, is strong willed, and will act accordingly. If we help young people realize the importance of their thoughts and actions, if instead of fear we teach them respect and love for themselves and each other, we will beat all the odds which now seem stacked against mankind. We can change the world by changing ourselves.

Native students might seem lazy in a class of thirty where the children of new immigrants study day and night or sports-oriented youths on teams fight to win. Native youngsters do not think it is important to compete and get straight A's, but have you ever seen a Native child torturing a cat or needlessly breaking tree branches? They are taught by their elders to respect everything in nature. They don't think they own the land and rule everything on it like white people do. They do not think the animals, the plants and the minerals were given to us 'higher beings' by God to serve us.

Unlike the Indian way that respects the spirits of the trees, plants, animals and stones, the Christian religion has taught us for centuries that we are the only creatures with a soul. Feeling superior to nature has led us to the brink of extinction. One culture's belief in its superiority over another - in ideas, beliefs, way of life and physical features - has resulted in centuries of devastating wars.

The Christian religion can no longer teach a child that it is the 'only truth'. Children now grow up knowing Hindus, Sikhs, Buddhists, and others who do not belong to any organized religion, all of whom model important human virtues.

The government cannot protect the new generation from war and from pollution. Schools fail to motivate youth to learn and parents are pre-occupied with their life problems and fail to pay attention to the psychological needs of adolescents. And all these problems pale beside the troubles of those who are abused physically or sexually.

What can we do to help children grow up to be responsible citizens, loving parents, and healthy, positive human beings? A lot! We can do a lot! We can teach young people to think - to think for themselves. Meeting one person who believes in you and in your ability to take charge of your own life can change your whole future. It takes only one. It could be a friend, a teacher, a parent, a social worker, or even a priest.

Instead of facts and rules and conclusions we should teach children to keep their minds open. Our education system overloads students with information. Only a creative mind can use information. In the present academic framework, students do not truly learn to 'think'. Yet creative thinking is the key to everything.

Reading is a higher level skill than watching television or following a computer's instructions. In the last two, all needed information is supplied to the user. The skill of reading must be acquired by the reader through thoughtful effort.

Information is useful for developing the mind, but only if the student is hungry for it. Nobody can gain knowledge and wisdom by memorizing. Actual experience, personal observations, and voluntary reading teach more than presenting facts.

Students watching television can't ask for explanations and can't exchange ideas with the speaker. Teachers and parents who lecture their children without sitting down and listening seriously to their responses do not teach anything. It is realistic to estimate that, in a class of thirty teenagers, only one-third will hear what the teacher says, even if everybody looks attentive.

Nobody can have any control over another person's mind. The class will learn almost nothing unless you engage them in conversation and inspire them to tell you what they think about the presented topic. Not much learning is acquired in a classroom where students sit in deadly silence, no matter how well controlled the class is. I support the teacher who leads his students into fiery arguments and encourages them to express opinions and even disagreements with the teacher. Teachers are not authorities; they are facilitators of learning.

Learning in general is a lifelong process. It is not confined to schools. We are learning and constantly re-evaluating what we know from birth to death. If we inspire our young people to become independent thinkers, they will have learned the most important tool they need to lead productive lives.

Some people will go through life satisfied with superficial knowledge. Others will go more deeply into their line of interest to understand the information. Regardless of the chosen route, everybody's personal truths undergo constant reassessment throughout their life. Thinking evolves with the person and the passing years.

Values that seem important in childhood change. There are no 'facts' that hold up forever. Social conditions evolve and the golden values of fifty years ago, such as 'Live and die for your country', now sound chauvinistic and dangerous.

Do not turn to government, churches, parents, or schools for leadership. Trust your own independent thinking. It is the most important tool you have to survive in the twenty-first century.

•••

CHAPTER XXVIII

•••

"Can I hide in your storage room, Ms. H?" asked Rob after everybody left. "They are looking for me to beat me up."

"Who are they?" I asked.

"I can't tell you. If I fink on them they promised to kill me."

You have to take these threats seriously, since these kind of fights can lead to tragic consequences.

Most school fights are started by bullies or gangs, a small portion of the student population. A sad group of confused and angry kids. They want attention by showing off in front of their peers. They are insecure kids who, in order to mask their fears, gang up with other insecure kids to feel strong and powerful.

I drove Rob home that day and a few days after. He solved his problem in the long run by staying in my art room until I cleaned up and all the students went home. Rob was refined, feminine, talented in many ways and obviously gay. He sat with the girls in the art room, happily chatting in girl talk. During Grade 10, he came out of the closet and told his parents. That day he came to my room after school and said, "I have nowhere to go Mrs. H., my parents kicked me out."

I did not want to believe this, since Rob's parents seemed to be caring and loving towards their children. Unfortunately, they decided to withdraw their support until Rob would 'smarten up'.

Rob lived in my house for two to three weeks, occupying one of my spare bedrooms. During this time I talked to the counselors and to the police until we found a family who took him in to help with their wheelchair-bound daughter. She was a student who attended the same art class as Rob did and they became good friends. His parents didn't sign papers so Rob couldn't get government help. They held out and said he could come home when he smartened up.

Rob never went home. He was old enough to make his own decisions. Last time I saw him he was working downtown and shared an apartment with friends. Fortunately, he did not slide into depression or become suicidal. He remained optimistic, balanced and cheerful.

The city cleared the area around the school for new housing development. They cleared the forest and built affordable homes attracting immigrant families in great numbers.

The new students with limited or no English, have been enrolled in ESL (English as a Second Language) classes and took Math, Music and Art, where they could succeed without speaking. They tend to sit in groups and spend the lunch break with their own cultural groups, speaking their mother tongue.

Racism arises from ignorance and lack of education, so I invented several art projects based on the colourful ethnic backgrounds of my students to teach cross-cultural understanding. The art room was full every lunchtime with teenagers finding refuge from bullying or homophobic harassments. This gave me the idea to start a Multicultural Club and give voice and a homebase for the underdogs. I started this group in 1980 and this became the best move of my teaching career.

We had weekly meetings to discuss issues and I listened intently to the young people. The club organized ethnic art shows and celebrated each others' religious holidays.

Over the next 20 years, the group grew into a powerful youth action club. We became experts with multicultural events; such as Global Fair, ethnic fashion show, diversity week, Mosaic Nights and Multicultural Weeks, when we invited speakers to our school to give workshops which made students realize the hurt that racism causes. One of the most successful programs was the Student Panel on Racism, where young people talked about their first experiences arriving in Canada.

By the early 90s the Club had 60-80 members and it was popular to belong. Student leaders, academic high achievers, sports stars and student council members joined other students who were using the art room as a safe place.

These students had their ideas about 'how to save the world' and started right there in our school by organizing paper and pop can recycling, even composting. Their interest in world affairs grew over the years. The club became a youth chapter for Amnesty International, sponsored students for education in the developing countries, attended conferences and volunteered in the community to work with the disabled. They collected clothes for street people and blankets for the animal shelters. Since erasing racism was not the only focus of the action programs, we renamed the group Global Issues Club.

I personally grew with them. My own teenage desire to 'save the world' came back with the powerful realization that I can do my share by sponsoring, initiating and organizing year-round events, putting students' attention on global and local concerns and helping them find positive solutions.

Some of my colleagues couldn't understand why I was spending countless extra hours, evenings, even weekends taking teenagers to conferences or practicing and rehearsing future events.

I felt like a while elephant in the staff room listening to some of my colleagues complaining about the workload or the behaviour of their students. Consequently I rarely spent time there and never ate my lunch in the cafeteria's secluded teacher's luncheon room. I spent those hours with my bright, interesting, enthusiastic students or sat in the privacy of my little office with individuals who needed my advice, encouragement or a sympathetic ear to listen to their problems.

One day I attended a conference entitled "Shared Vision". It was organized by a group of teachers whose goal was to teach peace and global awareness.

At this conference I met people who saw the role of teacher as I did. We talked the same language and I made lifelong friends. I joined their organization: The Peace and Global Education provincial specialist association.

Finding P.A.G.E. gave me wings. Over the years I served on the Executive as member-at-large, Vice President, President, Past President and presently membership chair. In our meetings we share ideas and motivate each other. We offer yearly conference retreats for teachers in a natural setting, holding the workshops in campgrounds where we can relax beside the fire, sleep in cabins, walk in nature and connect with each other.

It is important to rejuvenate and recharge the energy of teachers for the benefit of the young people they teach. After all, the future will depend on how they will think and act when they will be adults.

Teaching basic human values is one of the goals of the global educator's values, values which do not interfere with any religious or personal beliefs of individuals. Let's face it, for a long time teachers have been afraid to teach anything beyond the subject matter. We learned to respect other people's views on religion, politics or life philosophies and refrained to express our own.

Teenagers need answers to their questions and need help and guidance to develop a good self-image. Whether teachers like it or not, they influence pupils in a positive or negative way according to their actions. There are eternal values and truths such as respect, forgiveness and compassion which are infiltrated into our heart and give ground feed the human spirit.

Educators with this goal started the Virtues Project which was implemented in many elementary schools. Somehow the global consciousness brings about ideas at the same time in many communities.

While I was planning to work out a proposal to teach values from K to 12, Diane Tillman in California started the 'Living Values Education Program', providing excellent lesson plans for Kindergarten teachers to University professors. Her workshops are now breaking ground in many countries all over the world and I cheer for their success from the bottom of my heart.

To help the P.A.G.E. group sponsor informational lectures and several day training sessions for the interested, I retired in the year 2000 and cannot try it myself, but my global educator friends who implemented the Living Values exercises in their teaching materials are reporting great success — fewer problems with discipline, bullying, homophobia and racism.

•••
CHAPTER XXIX
•••

Canada is the forerunner for the future, our multiracial society modeling world global citizenship. Our government encourages people to celebrate diversity by supporting ethnic arts, culture and history. Canada grants equal rights to everybody.

We can see what separation of ethnic groups creates in other parts of the world. Tribalism, ethnic cleansing, genocides, terrorist acts by religious extremists and the sad list goes on.

Oneness of mankind and the realization of it, is the vision of many. There is only one race - the human race. Where can we start to achieve this, if not in our immediate surroundings, in our family, our community?

My effort to bring the different groups together within our school to work, to play, to create an anti-racial environment, paid off greatly with the Global Issues Club.

The following are direct statements from students. They gave me permission to include their real names.

Cindy Quack, 1995 (Background Vietnamese)

"Having been born and raised until the age of 8 in a small town in Southern Vietnam, I experienced living from day-to-day in extreme poverty. After immigrating to Canada I felt shock, depression, fear, confusion and a lot of discrimination. This led me to develop anorexia soon after I arrived. Despite this difficult start of my life, I eventually overcame the eating disorder and developed fluency in English within one year. The same year I received a citizenship award 'for one outstanding student showing the most courage, sportsmanship and school pride'.

I joined the Multicultural Club because I wanted to be part of a team that makes a positive influence on the student body. I was attracted to the club because I had heard that they sponsored children in third world countries. Since I wanted to do the same thing, but couldn't afford the money, I thought this would be a great way for me to contribute. I also wanted to meet other young people who had the same goals and concerns about the future of our planet as myself. Through the Multicultural Club, I have developed a sense of belonging, acceptance and the confidence and courage to actively participate in events and speak up for global issues."

Because I was raised in Vietnam and in Canada I have grown up experiencing a variety of customs. This has enriched my life and has made me become very interested in learning more about the many different cultures that are out there. I have also attended Multicultural Youth Forums, where I learned how to be a role model for my peers and how to advocate cross cultural interactions while participating in activities which create a positive future and celebrate racial harmony."

Cindy graduated from high school at the end of the 94/95 school year and has kept in touch with me. She just received her bachelor degree in biochemistry and was accepted at a Toronto college to become a Naturopathic Physician.

Fainuma Axad, 1995 (Background Fijian)
"The Multicultural Club is a club which involves all races and all nationalities. Yes, there's a thing called multilingualism, in which I believe. I believe that today in this society if we young people don't make a difference, then who will? (The reason I joined the multicultural club is to make difference in the world.) Racism is a question in all our minds. I think that each and every one should make an effort to erase racism. There are so many unique cultures in our society. We should accept others as they are instead of hating a person because of a difference in colour or culture. I want to make a difference and tell everyone that hatred towards others gets us absolutely nowhere. Learn to love, not hate!"

The following was written by Fainuma and the previous student, Cindy:

> "*Violence and Alienation.*
> *Dear B.C. Teachers,*
> *Our biggest concern regarding political issues is gangs in schools. The reason for gangs is that we are brought up in a dysfunctional society. If parents were more involved with their child's social life, this would make children feel more wanted, so they wouldn't want to be involved in gangs.*
> *If students, parents, teachers and other educators have better communication between one another, this will contribute to a better and safer environment.*"

Fainuma was raised in a loving, supportive, traditional Muslim family. Right after graduation she was married in a pre-arranged traditional way. I was invited to the wedding. It was one of my most unforgettable experiences. Fainuma's mother dressed me in one of her saris, long gold earrings and make up. I was transferred into a world I usually experienced only by reading National Geographic articles.

Unfortunately her marriage failed. She divorced and became a dental assistant. Recently she invited me to see her newborn daughter from her second marriage. Fainuma's beautiful smile and shiny dark eyes expressed happiness. She is one example of many who were raised in a traditional way but found balance between the old ways and the new.

Anne Marie Khouri, 1995 (Background Lebanese)

"I am a sixteen-year-old female who has more than one concern about the world in which she is living. There are so many problems with society these days that it is amazing to me that people can sleep at night. My goal in life is to educate and attempt to solve these global issues. As a member of the Multicultural Club at my high school, I feel that I am getting one step closer to accomplishing my goal. In the club all of our races are united as one. We have helped and saved many lives, and only wish to do more. The most fascinating aspect of this club is that our members put aside their differences in order to unite and create a very strong, devoted

*and successful race: the human race. Hopefully others can
learn from us and begin to solve some of society's problems.
Together we can survive any battle. Peace, love and hope."*

Anne Marie worked at the Attorney General's office after graduation. She was a youth coordinator for the Lower Mainland Youth Action Groups. Presently she is studying at SFU to become a high school teacher. Good luck my priceless, bright, beautiful daughter. You will be an awesome teacher planting seeds for the future.

Parminder Johal, 1995 (Background Indian)

*"I felt like I was the only one who was offended by racism,
sexism, stereotype, prejudice and discrimination; the only
one who was worried, scared and frustrated about the state
of our world; the only youth who cared about children (the
same age as me) who were fighting for their lives in other
countries. However, this changed when I became a member
of the Global Issues Club at Johnston Heights. Everyone in
this club (teachers, sponsors and students) share the same
feelings concerning problems that our world is facing. In
each member of the Global Issues Club, I have found a
friend for a lifetime and I know that through our courage,
cooperation, devotion, loyalty and concern, we are coming
closer to making the world a better place. Peace, love, joy
and sunshine."*

Today Parminder is a social worker but wants to get more into politics. She wrote the ASAT exam and started law school in September 2001.

Sandy Cheung, 1993, (Background Chinese)

*"Dear Teachers, There have been several fights that I know
of involving teenagers of different races. They might believe
that violence can solve problems and allow them to show
power over one another, but something must have started
the fire. Is it racism? Is it people's ignorance that leads them
to discriminate against the ones who are not identical to
themselves?*

*The communication gap between one race and another
created by racism causes misunderstanding, mistrust,*

*hatred, confrontation and can lead to violent acts. Worst
of all, racist attitudes can be passed on from one person to
another.*

*Therefore, if possible, children should be taught not to dis-
criminate against others through activities supported by
their teachers and their parents. Since teenagers should be
mature enough to interpret the flaw of racism, having a
multiculturalism unit in a Social Studies Course is very
reasonable. This unit would give teenagers information
about different cultures, and this increases the speed of
acceptance of cultural differences and reduces racism effectively. Also, because Social Studies is a required course for
high school graduation, students are guaranteed to have the
lessons taught to them. However, if the course is optional,
students may show less interest in it even before they have
taken the course. Hopefully, you the reader, will aggressively
participate in anti-racism programs and be able to provide
valuable suggestions about this concern that I and many
others have."*

I lost contact with Sandy, but I hope she carried her fighting spirit into her life's
work after graduation.

Inez Joere, 1993 (Background Peruvian-Belgian)

*"In ancient Greece, where the foundations for modern
democracy were laid, the Greeks gathered in their forum to
discuss what was best for their polis, their city.
One thousand years ago society was basically agricultural.
Today we are faced with the consequences of the industrial
revolution. Society and politics are more complicated.*

*Like it or not, our generation will have to present solutions
to these problems because now it is not just a case of losing
the support of one group or gaining support of another, it is
a matter of survival.*

*As young adults we can achieve more now if we would
only realize our power in the political realm. We are the*

voters for future elections and we must use that fact to our advantage by putting pressure on political candidates and the power groups that influence them. We can participate in economic embargoes on manufacturers of certain products. The only limitation we have is our numbers. Action is only effective, on a larger scale, if we have a large number of people to work with.

Presently, Inez is a freelance writer and frequently comes to my home to discuss personal and world issues.

Andrea Mau, 2001 (Background: Born in India to Chinese parents)

"During the first Global Issues Club meeting, I remember saying to myself, "This is exactly where I want to be." Ms. Hittrich's constant motivation and determination inspired me to become part of the 'big picture'. Every activity that we participated in shed some new light on the various ethnic backgrounds in the world. However, the Multicultural Camp of 1998 was the one that brought a major transition in my life. The different cultures that I was exposed to really helped me appreciate others and converted me to someone who wanted to make a difference. I transpired into an active member helping out with all the events that were a part of our dynamic club. Through Ms. Hittrich's eyes, I began to see the world from a different perspective and learned my life's most valuable lesson — a small step can make a difference."

Presently, Andrea is taking Business Ed at UBC.

Vivian Tan, 2001, (Background Chinese)

"It is a privilege to be part of Beata's Global Issues Club at the school. Not only has it been my favourite high school extra-curricular activity, but an important method that has helped me expand my horizons. It is this club that has influenced me to think in an open-minded manner and enabled me to make wise decisions to help in the world. Through

this, I have become a different person. My self-esteem and confidence have developed miraculously. Though our club was small, it has made tremendous progress in making a difference in our community. It made me realize that young individuals like myself can help shape our planet.

It is necessary to have non-profit organizations such as this club as a tool to educate, inspire and enlighten our youth to do something about the environment, human rights and personal development. This club has become a touchstone base for me, encouraging me to promote cultural diversity, protect the environment and improve the lives of other people. This is only the beginning. I believe that if humanity unites and reasons together in a civilized manner, peace can prevail."

Vivian Tan is a college student, studying art with the goal of being an animation artist.

Upasana Ochani, 2001 (Background Indian)

"I think the hardest part of being a human being in today's world is empathizing with other fellow human beings and appreciating each for what it is — a very precious living entity. This weakness has also been prevalent in me. As a teenager it was very hard for me to look beyond myself. To realize that the world did not begin and end with me, that I am part of a bigger picture....where things like food, clean air and water, things we take for granted keep all of us alive. Participating in the activities of The Global Issues Club proved to be a real eye opener for me.

This experience has nurtured in me an ability to feel in a very selfless way and think from a collective perspective of 'us' and not simply an individual one of 'me;.

The future generations who follow us deserve to breathe clean air, drink uncontaminated water and eat organic fruits and vegetables. It should be one of our highest priorities to work together to tackle global warming and to ban all products that are produced in a manner which damages our fragile environment.

I aspire to learn skills in Human Resources Management as I pursue my studies so that I can reach out to people in developing countries who have the potential and the resources but are not receiving the support they need and deserve. My goal is to implement effective and useful methods in organizations to help individuals make a difference in their communities. The Global Issues Club has ignited a desire in me to take action and not just feel remorse for this planet and its people."

EPILOGUE

Every road comes to an end. In June, 2000 I had to walk out from the art room. Retirement is mandatory when you reach the age of 65. Was I ready? Hardly, to tell the truth.

The outpouring of attention and love I was showered with by my students, the Global Issues Club and by my colleagues made it easier to close the door and open a new chapter in my life.

In the summer I sat down and planned several workshops for youth of all ages. It was important for me to keep in touch with teaching. Also, I made a list of wonderful activities I could pursue with my suddenly available time. I never had a problem with boredom, since there are so many meaningful and interesting things to do. Still, when September arrived and my daughter, who is a teacher now, headed toward the first day of school, I hugged her with tears in my eyes.

Oh, I got busy — exercise, gardening, writing, cooking, socializing, reading all the books I didn't have time to read before and giving workshops. Regardless, I went into a slight depression, missing the daily contact with my beloved teenagers.

When I was invited to speak about peace to a class of Grade 8 students in Victoria, I had to fight back my tears. All those fresh, shining faces were looking forwards and I, the old teacher, was standing in the front of a class again. What an unforgettable moment of realization — that if I was born to be a teacher, I will die like one.

Since I regained the rest of life and beat the depression without pills, I tore up the prescription of anti-depressants that my doctor had prescribed. I told myself that I can get high on life without any chemicals. I was right.

As my days and months rolled on in retirement I found satisfaction organizing conferences for teachers and for youth. I served time as the directors of charitable organizations and began getting invitations from schools to work with kids in elementary and in high schools.

Looking back on my long years of teaching, I have a good feeling about my role. Of course I made several mistakes and was not on top of every situation. Sometimes I overacted or made the wrong remark, but my overall never-faltering, genuine love toward people helped to sail over troubled waters. Students understood that I really cared and responded with respect and love.

A half century has passed since I started to teach folk dance and ballet in Hungary. Over 50 years I have worked with children, adults and mostly teenagers.

I feel blessed to have been able to touch the lives of thousands of students as they certainly touched my life.

I liked challenges in my life. To solve them made me feel alive and successful. Now I am facing the challenge of old age. To deal with it I want to stay active, interested in current events and be a useful member of society.

I like the indigenous people's view on aging and consider myself an elder instead of old. The Western image of old age is anything but appealing.

Yes, sometimes I feel that my body can't keep up with my spirit, so I slow down and give myself the luxury of rest. I spend more time in solitude, meditate and exercise regularly to keep my body, mind and spirit healthy.

My love toward teenagers has never faded away. Young people visit me regularly and ask for my advice or encouragement. Several of my former students have become personal friends —they say I inspire them. I feel very rich with their trust and love.

As I come to the end of the story of my teaching career, my grandchildren are starting high school and the challenge of teenage years. My goal is to be their friend and help them through those turbulent years with my unconditional love.

I am optimistic about the future, those dark years when I started my journey are well in the past.

Today we teach young people to be independent thinkers instead of living in blind obedience. If life changed so much for the better in the last 50 years, how much will it improve in the next century? We must project positive thoughts forward while working for a better world. Do not wait for others to change, start with yourself. Walk your talk.

Fill you heart with love, replacing fears and if you work with young people in any vocation or you are parents of teenagers, give them personal attention, listen, speak as if you are speaking to a friend, do not preach. They will respect you if you give them respect, after all, every human being hungers for attention and love.

ISBN 1-41204910-5